For Jackie and [?] dear friends and compadres!

Conservation Writing

Essays at the Crossroads of Nature and Culture

by

Luke Wallin

with love,

Luke Wallin

May 28, 2008

A Center for Policy Analysis Book
University of Massachusetts Dartmouth

ISBN-13: 978-0-9790276-0-4
ISBN-10: 0-9790276-0-8

Published by the Center for Policy Analysis,
University of Massachusetts Dartmouth
85 Old Westport Road
North Dartmouth, MA. 02747-2300.
http://www.umassd.edu/cfpa/

Cover paintings by Mary Elizabeth Gordon
Cover design by Melissa Page Jones (Mdesign)

CONTENTS

To

Mary Elizabeth Gordon

Acknowledgements

"River of Silence": was revised from a version in the anthology *High Horse*, Fleur de Lis Press, 2005, originally published in the journal BAILE, University College Dublin, Spring 1998.

"Metaphors that Haunt American Landscapes" grew from the talk "Myths, Models and Environmental Metaphors," presented at the fall 1990 annual meeting of the New England Popular Culture Association, Amherst, Massachusetts.

"John Muir writing 'God's Fine Wilderness'" was revised from "Writing 'God's Fine Wilderness': John Muir in the Mountains of California," in *Nature And Identity In Cross-Cultural Perspective*, edited by Anne Buttimer and Luke Wallin, Kluwer Academic Publishers, 1999.

"Science Journalism Basics: A Woodcock Singing Ground" was revised from a version in Little Compton Landscapes, The Sakonnet Preservation Association's newsletter, 2000.

"Creative Nonfiction: Sharing Sacred Ground" was revised from the version in *Far from Home*, an anthology of father-daughter travel adventure stories, edited by Wendy Knight, published June 2004 by Seal Press.

"Five Kinds of Environmental Writing" was revised from "Environmental Writing and Minority Education," in *Voices In English Classrooms: Honoring Diversity And Change, Classroom Practices In Teaching English*, Vol. 28, edited by Lenora Cook and Helen C. Lodge, published by The National Council of Teachers of English Press, Spring 1996.

"Imagining a Balance of Nature" was revised from "Science and the Paradox of Harmony," a review essay discussing three books on science and environment, published in UnderCurrents, York University, Ontario, Oct. 1996.

Parts of "Conservation's Observer Problem" and "Choosing Landscape Values" appeared in Little Compton Landscapes, the newsletter of the Sakonnet Preservation Association, 2000.

"Two Interpretations of Leopold's Land Ethic" was revised from the talk "Two Rhetorical Paths to Conservation," presented to the Humanities Program and the Law School, James Cook University, Townsville, Australia, August 2002.

Introduction

For places in need of conservation, a writer's fresh metaphor — properly contextualized and scientifically unpacked — can enable dramatic success. Take Rachel Carson's 'web of life,' which elegantly joined 'web,' with its connotations of structural engineering, to 'life,' with its organic associations. This powerful figure of speech helped launch the environmental movement of the 1960s. Or consider Marjory Stoneman Douglas's 'river of grass,' which gave compressed, lyrical expression to the mysterious riverine dynamics of Florida's everglades, and sparked the everglades protection movement of the 1940s. By examining textual moments when conservation writers broke through conventional views to reveal the fluid world, a writer can grow in craft and wisdom. Carson was a scientist first, and she understood the implications of a 'lifeweb' before she discovered the lyrical words; Douglas was a writer, and her felicitous phrase 'river of grass' somewhat accidentally pointed the way to seeing the everglades as an extension of the Miami River. These two cases illustrate the shifting ground between science and persuasion, between fact and lyricism.

These inventive moments prompt the question: Can a conservationist develop a personal approach to writing which will increase the odds of influence? Can such an approach integrate ecological understanding and artistic process? The blending effort is worthwhile, for effective writing must be more than lyrical, and biology must be more than technically correct articles in academic journals if it is to serve conservation goals.

A conservation writer requires the knowledge scientific ecology can offer about a specific place, but also a sense of an audience with the power to protect local values. The writer requires research, yet no amassing of data alone can produce an emotionally moving document which will engage the will to conserve. For this, a writer needs immersion in subject, to the point where creative connections between concepts and words take place on an unconscious level, then emerge on the page as raw, first-draft surprises. In other words, beyond science and textual analysis, the conservation writer requires a commitment, and a process like that of the literary storyteller, the creative writer.

All sorts of cultural divisions mitigate against this understanding. Science is taught separately from writing, and is thought objective in contrast to writing's subjectivity. Ecological science is written in the form of impersonal, technical narratives about data points, deviation curves, and average behaviors. Nature writing, on the other hand, typically features an 'I' or narrative consciousness and frames encounter stories about animals, landscapes or seascapes that are deliciously unique. In educational background as well as professional funding pressures, scientists learn to look past colorful anecdotal behavior at species norms expressed in graphs and formulae. Meanwhile creative writers learn to coax their childhood memories and dreams into consciousness, and then treat these as starting points for imaginative invention. With such different concepts about education and practice, it's no wonder that scientists and writers often experience uneasy longings for each other's skills.

At the heart of every conservation project lies a piece of writing which describes the land's values, lays out threats, and proposes solutions. Whether the scale of conservation is a beach or wetland, a town's watershed or a bioregional ecosystem, each stage of the conservation process requires intelligent, passionate writing. Someone must express the landscape's meaning for current residents. This task is always challenging and fresh, because landscapes and people change, and because old language grows awkward and clichéd. New generations need to see — through resonant texts — their land as they feel it, and as it reflects their identities.

Writers apply creative techniques to such forms as the nature essay (which increases appreciation for places), environmental reporting (which informs about threats), and the community plan (which recommends protective actions). In applying creative skills to conservation forms, a writer needs to know something about the science of ecology, concepts of landscape beauty, and the history of environmental ethics. Each of the thirteen essays here seeks to illuminate interwoven strands of culture and nature, either by example or discussion.

Essay One, "River of Silence," displays the Nature Writing genre, with its emphasis on journey and invitational description. A report on my conservation team's exploration of the Connecticut River, it was written as prelude to drafting a protection plan.

Two, "Metaphors that Haunt American Landscapes," examines four metaphor families that have played great roles in American thinking about nature and culture.

Three, "John Muir writing 'God's Fine Wilderness,'" considers Muir's writing with an eye to discovering why his work was so effective.

Four, "Science Journalism Basics: A Woodcock Singing Ground," presents a piece I wrote for a land trust newsletter. I introduce it with a commentary on elements which environmental journalism shares with other forms, from persuasive op/ed columns to nature essays and community plans. I discuss strategies for each element.

Five, "Creative Nonfiction: Sharing Sacred Ground," tells the story of taking my daughter Eva to my woods and trying to share my traditions with her. It's similar to a nature essay, but more focused on human conflict and drama; it uses invitational description as a technique for encouraging readers to care for a natural place. This care, if the description is done properly, should transcend differences like the ones between Eva and me.

Six, "Five Kinds of Environmental Writing," exhibits a variety of forms through which a writer can explore relations between self and nature.

Essays Seven through Nine discuss ways to integrate ecological with writing knowledge, at a scale which allows a writer to influence a community.

Essays Ten through Thirteen explore philosophical issues that arise in framing conservation documents and presenting a foundation for a conservation case. The framework here is pragmatic, and anti-foundationalist, in the technical sense. However, I argue that this position does not entail relativism. The debate within environmental ethics over this issue mirrors the national debate over fundamentalism. Some argue that, without their claims to absolute knowledge, there is no basis for moral behavior. One hears such positions from so-called representatives of religions, often serving as justification for warfare. In the conservation field, fear of relativism is expressed by such statements as "if wilderness isn't holy, bearing intrinsic value, then a developer's claim is equal to anyone else's." But to begin with the moral conclusion we want, and work backward to the foundation in epistemology and ontology that would secure it, is both dishonest and unnecessary. It is one thing to feel the holy character of a wild place, and another to analyze the language through which writers express it. Muir and Leopold are sometimes cited as examples, almost beyond criticism, of writers who spoke the truth of holy nature, and laid down proper metaphors for its respect and even worship. But close reading of their work reveals sophisticated understandings of the language of nature, and of the audience appeals likely to generate conservation support.

Consideration of environmental philosophy, in this book at least, is meant to explore the ways effective conservation requires storytelling about places, in addition to merely listing natural and cultural resources as elements in a text. These stories should avoid clichés, and create new metaphors and other tropes which capture ways people value places. The discovery of fresh metaphors happens within a creative writing process, unconsciously and well as consciously; it's a process enriched by a writer's training, in addition to rhetorical and scientific knowledge. Ecological knowledge must be gained through working with scientists, planners and citizens with experience of the land and its creatures. Becoming a conservation writer requires solitary practice similar to that of the poet or fictionist, plus reading about persuasion and ecology; but there the solitude ends, and group participation must begin.

The essays in this collection reflect my attempts to integrate writing, scientific learning, and practical planning experiences. I grew up in a conservation-minded family in rural Mississippi, where my father established the first tree farm in our county. As early as 1950 he taught me the evils of clear cutting, and the need to balance interests of humans and wild animals. During college summers I worked for the Forest Service in Idaho, fighting fires, clearing mountainsides and manning a lookout tower. In college and graduate school I studied Philosophy; I wrote an M.A. thesis on how language refers to the world. Then I took a Master of Fine Arts degree from the Iowa Writer's Workshop, and eventually published eight works of fiction, many with environmental themes. Later I earned a graduate degree in Regional Planning, and participated in conservation projects in the deep South, New England, and France. I worked with a land trust in Rhode Island, and as a Professor of English at the University of Massachusetts Dartmouth developed a range of courses in writing about nature and culture. As Visiting Fulbright Professor at University College Dublin I participated in a Ph.D. seminar taught by Anne Buttimer, Professor and Chair of the Geography Department. This led to our co-editing and contributing to the book *Nature and Identity in Cross-Cultural Perspective*, in which twenty authors examine the interwoven concepts of nature and identity in their countries. As a Senior Research Associate at the Center for Policy Analysis, I have worked on integrating conservation writing into policy studies. As a faculty member in the Spalding University Master of Fine Arts in Writing Program, I have explored representations of nature in creative nonfiction, fiction, and writing for children. These experiences have been a lot of fun, and along the way have suggested strategies for conservation writers.

There are practical tips in this book, but it's mainly a series of conversations with my reader as I imagine him or her: writing, absorbing ecosystem knowledge, and making decisions. Writers plan their stories, but discover surprises as unconscious processes take over during composition. Conservationists juxtapose scientific information, cultural claims, and personal desires for diversity and beauty as they create stories of protection for natural places. The strongest conservation writing doesn't just illustrate planning, it brings an artistic process to the creation of ecological plans.

One

River of Silence

We slip our canoes into the Connecticut as clouds of spirit-mist rise from its cool surface. We're just below Turners Falls dam, near the Massachusetts-Vermont line, and this surface fog seems strangely alive. The Indians once saw in these whitish movements the ghostly residents of a place, and this morning as we slide past sandbar willows out into the current and breeze, that vision feels true.

This site — Peskeompscut, to the local Potumtucks — was the scene of a terrible massacre in 1676. English colonials surprised sleeping villagers and destroyed 100 people: children and "many old men and women." Another 140 died leaping over the falls, or when their attackers followed along the shore and shot them as they swam. I wonder whether these souls are among the spirits rising from the river's silvery surface on this perfect fall morning.

There are ten of us in four canoes. Nine are members of a University of Massachusetts Amherst team charged with preservation strategy and tactics. The tenth is our leader, Terry Blunt, a trim, quiet intense man of about 35. Terry is a Senior Planner for the Commonwealth, and his first lesson to us was about language.

"Don't use the word 'preservation'," he said. "It

makes people mad. More than mad, furious. 'Conservation' is all right, but the best word is 'protection'."

We have taken this deeply to heart. We are to formulate a plan for our study area, Reach II of the Connecticut River in Massachusetts, stretching from the Vermont line down to the town of Northampton. It is the last free-flowing section of the river within the Commonwealth, and Terry wants to safeguard its quiet values before the region's development craze overwhelms them.

We make good speed over the water, and our bowman, John Bennett, maneuvers us closer to Terry's canoe to hear his soft commentary. Terry is pointing high above us as an elegant osprey, flashing its brown and white feathers, shoots upriver in the sunlight. Just a few years ago the river was terribly polluted and all the osprey had vanished. But new laws have brought better waste treatment plants to the river towns, and the fish are once again fit to eat. Osprey seem to have heard the news; they've returned in healthy numbers and become a symbol of valley pride.

Terry indicates a pipe protruding from a high bank, streaming liquid down into the current. "That's why I'm here," John Bennett says to me as we paddle past. John is a powerful young man in his mid-twenties; he is handsome, self-contained and practical. "I was working for the state as an inspector. I'd visit all these plants and they'd show me how they'd sealed off their pipes. They'd claim they were doing proper disposal, not dumping anymore. But you could look at the valves and tell they were lying. You could look in their eyes and tell. I knew it and they knew I knew."

Terry motions us over to the east bank, where we hold all four canoes together, bobbing, as he shows us a deposit of thick blue clay. "The old Indians liked this," he says, "it works beautifully in pots." And then he gives us another warning: "Please don't anybody tell where this vein lies. We don't need people digging out the side of the bank, undercutting the ledge."

I look up to tall maples and oaks in fall colors, and at the steep eroded slope laced with poison ivy. It is amazing that people would destroy this bank, that we must hold the secret of the blue clay.

For the past few years I've researched and written books involving endangered species and Native American culture. The aim of my books has been art, not action. Joining this project has given me a sense of how people can combine skills in conservation work and make things happen. But the first lessons, it seems, are restraint, study, care, silence.

The man in the middle of my canoe is Chris Ryan. He learned to make maps in the army, and now produces limited editions for conservation groups. His work is first-rate, and I have proposed to him that we collaborate on a book which would identify all the ancient tribal territories in Massachusetts, and provide maps and directions to each. When the traveler arrives, there will be a local path to a special place — an overlook, a grove, a waterfall. We would choose each spot by our sense of sacred place, and give the visitor a chance to experience what the old tribes might have most appreciated.

Toward this end, as well as the Reach II project, I've been visiting with Bob Paynter, archaeologist at the University of Massachusetts Amherst. He's been considering my request for site information.

But he has given me second thoughts with a story.

There's a man in Greenfield who specializes in looting Indian graves and middens. He absorbs the rumors of a new discovery, and he'll bore like a coal miner, like a human mole. Once he went underground from a neighbor's property, and tunneled all the way into an incredible site. He looted it, broke pots, took the bones of the dead. This man is the link between an international artifact-trading network, and the places we want to protect.

As the canoes bob in the current and Terry reminds us of our vow of silence about the vein of blue clay, I wonder whether the sacred-places book would only invite the least spiritual among us. For that matter, will our efforts at a protection plan only draw more visitors to this fragile river?

But when we slide into the current again, and the wind picks up, clean fresh air drives some of my doubts away. Whether it's negative ions or benevolent spirits, I believe in our mission.

We paddle in a long, lazy curve and the banks are timbered with thick beeches and maples. Straight, impressive hemlocks rise in a shadow-dark wall atop the bluff. There is no clear sign of humanity, of farming or building, though we have learned this wildness is an illusion of the river. The entire valley has been intensely farmed for centuries, and now only a narrow band of forest graces the banks. But these enclosing trees and bluffs give a sense of timeless peace. It is a quality we will claim in our report as a rare cultural memory: we are experiencing what New England river valleys were like five hundred years ago. Ralph Waldo Emerson, writing in 1835, declared that Smith and Jones may own their farms, but the view encompassing each of them belongs to everyone. And especially since Lady Bird Johnson, first lady to President Lyndon Johnson, held a white house conference on Scenic Beauty back in 1969, planners have been able to articulate vistas like this one as common property "visual resources," in Emerson's sense. There are systems of comparison, rank-ordering, quantification.

We come into sight of a pair of black cormorants, and watch them dive deep. The Dutch and Chinese trained these birds to retrieve fish from the sea, and ensured their return by placing brass rings around their necks. Only by returning could they earn an occasional fish, and be allowed to swallow. Such an old interaction between humans and birds brings to mind our mission. Our team is not outside the ecosystem of the river, far from it. What we accomplish may determine the fate of these birds, certainly of the ospreys and bald eagles. This winding, riverine landscape is both a

4

centuries-old, humanized site, a kind of grand public garden, and also a bit of wild nature in the midst of intense farming. I dip my fingers into the cold water as we shoot past the cormorants. A cluster of gray and white gulls bobs close to shore.

After an hour Terry motions for us to beach our canoes on a big sandbar up ahead, and soon we walk and stretch our backs. He instructs us to pull driftwood and stones into a rough circle. Once we are settled on these dry seats over the damp sand he shows us silver maples and a tall cottonwood on the bank. Here beside us grow limber saplings of sandbar cherry.

"Since the river cleanup, fish populations have become more stable," Terry says. "All year you have walleye, channel cat, northern pike, small and largemouth bass, rainbow trout, and pickerel. anadromous, or migrating, fish include sea lamprey, blueback herring, American shad, Atlantic salmon and short-nosed sturgeon. That last one's on the federally endangered list, and there's a $20,000 fine for possession."

"Now the water flow is a big factor for all these fish, especially herring and shad, and especially during spawning. Large fluctuations can sweep away fish eggs and larvae, or kill them through lack of oxygen. To keep things even, the Cabot Station hydro plant is required to release 14,000 cubic feet of water per second at all times."

This information stuns me. It brings home how utterly dependent all this river life is upon constant human monitoring and care. We literally have the Connecticut in our hands, and I pray some dial-watcher won't nod off, some lonely midnight.

Terry wants to limit powerboats to 10 miles per hour. This would give the shad better protection, and it's the sort of regulation the six river towns might agree to. He says common sense would tell us this is a sound idea, yet he can't get a biologist to testify seriously: there aren't data, no way to get any. The biologists, who met with us a few days ago, were chagrined by their professional codes. They didn't want motors in the reach at all. They said they know oil and gas spills, and props churning up the shallow bottom near the sandbars, can't possibly be good for spawning fish. What they don't know is how to close the gap between their concern and their science.

It is time for another secret. "Right up there," Terry says, "is an endangered-species habitat. Whatever you do, don't talk about this." We are alert. "*Crotalus horridus*," he says, "the timber rattlesnake."

There are cries of *eeeww*.

"It seems strange," he says, "but some folks would hunt them down, if they knew where to find them.

"The old males turn almost black. They're in demand in carnivals, and even for cowboy hatbands."

We talk a while longer, then fall silent and listen to the river. It speaks strongly and softly, flowing within its frame of banks and timber, carrying its strange mixture of wildlife and culture. It seems a long time before Terry rises and says, "well." And I am beginning to feel a belonging here, even to these recent strangers. Our task together feels less important than our canoe trip, at least right now. This feeling, called the "river effect," this sense of the possibility for quiet transit and learning, is precisely what we must protect.

Downstream we approach a site where Terry is on the brink of closing a deal to buy development rights. This is one of his — and our — most valuable preservation tools. Farmers who want to protect the scenic or wildlife or cultural values of their land, but who need cash and must face exaggerated land prices, can sell development rights but retain ownership. Many don't know how this works, so publicizing the process is one of our tasks.

But we mustn't tell anyone about the farm up ahead. Terry has been discussing the sale of development rights, and the farmer is most uncertain. Not only are negotiations at a delicate stage, but this river's edge is a small, fragile ecotone of rare plants. And again, there are those who, if they knew, would steal and market them.

The more I learn of the threats, the more amazed I am at the river's surviving richness, its wealth of life and history, its unspoiled timber and sandbars and long thin islands. Hedged in by the development boom in the valley, assaulted by looters, the river itself is coming to seem an island of sacred space in an urbanizing world.

I think of my friend Barry Greenbie, a professor of planning at the university who has an intriguing theory of cultural space. Barry canvassed decades of research on brain physiology, wondering whether this work could illuminate the human need for safe, comforting spaces. The ancient limbic system seems to require secure borders, nest sites, locally defined spaces to which we can attach emotional bonds and memories. But the outer cortex, a later phenomenon, gives us abstract thought and projects our concepts, grids and schemes, onto global, impersonal space. Some cultures, such as the Japanese, recognize this and provide for dual spatial experience. They allow stability and comfort within the home and walled garden, preserving tradition in this sphere, while encouraging innovation and change in the professional realm of global trade. Because the Japanese are so traditional, Barry contends, they are able to excel at the modern.

But when a culture represses this duality, the result is psychological disturbance; for example, densely crowded apartment buildings in the "international" style fail to give residents a clear inner/outer experience. As a result, there is no peace of mind for renewal, planning and creative struggle in the outside world.

It seems to me that Reach II of the Connecticut River is precisely a safe, bounded home territory for those valley residents whose working lives are spent amid increasing traffic, development and competition. Perhaps an argument

7

of this kind can be constructed within our project, perhaps not. But either way, this experience of the quiet river is a blessing. It may be natural habitat as well, for the ancient limbic brain.

We pass the spectacular Sunderland Cascades, huge water-worn boulders on the river's east bank, across which thin, glassy sheets of spring water pour. This is another site targeted for special protection, another in-process deal of which we team members must not speak. We glide past in admiration, and soon come into sight of our landing beneath the Sunderland bridge.

Our trip is over. There are good feelings as we drag the canoes up the muddy bank, and carry them to car top racks and pickup beds. I am tired as I wave goodbye to my new colleagues. My house is only one mile away, and in a few minutes I am home with my family, filled with images and sounds from the river.

My little boy, three and one-half, asks, "Did you save the river, Dad?"

I smile and meet his mother's eyes. His question reminds me that conservation is a daily effort.

"We made a start."

"Good," he says.

I drive them back down the road to the water's edge in the falling light, and we stand beside the empty landing. A kingfisher scoots upriver in its dipping pattern of flight, and a bat skims narrowly past my head.

My responsibility is to write the section of our report on Native American "cultural resources." And although Bob Paynter seems close to showing me the site files, he has almost begged me not to reveal where the arrowheads, pottery, and human bones lie. I began this assignment eagerly, thinking the best argument for protection would be a clear designation of the values at risk, of what could be lost without strong action. But I know now that I'll be writing for the looters of graves and rare plants, of blue clay and rattlesnakes, as well as for those with the will to preserve. I must convey a sense of Reach II's worth without compromising the choice locations, especially tribal sites. We must protect the graves; everywhere there is a storm of Indian demand for the return of ancestral remains. Many Native Americans say their ancestors' ghosts will walk the landscape, restless and weary, until their bones are finally consecrated in the proper ground.

Standing by the dark, gurgling river with my family, I believe I hear what the mist-spirits were telling me this morning. It is something to know the ancient riverside camps and middens and graves. These, Bob Paynter will tell me in time. He will unlock a dusty, unused room and show me the eyes-only site files. Some will indeed reveal sacred places, and if I visited them I would feel that, even now. But such secrets have no place in my report, nor in a guidebook of maps. I must take up, this time, the path of silence.

[The six river towns voted our protection plan into their zoning codes, giving it the status of law.]

Two

Metaphors that Haunt American Landscapes

One of the characteristics that makes humans so powerful is the capacity to assert that 'one thing is the same as another.' This ability allows us to remake the world through creativity, to invent and deny identities, and to find fresh language to express our feelings and hopes for the land. Once master metaphors are asserted, in phrases like 'nature is divine order,' 'nature is an organic creature,' or 'nature is a great machine,' they seem to take a life of their own for whoever thinks about them. They suggest endless corollaries to the unconscious as well as the conscious mind, and they deeply influence our feelings about ourselves in the world. Thus our sense of being-in-the world is partially created, and certainly reinforced, through the metaphors we use.

As the following sections show, environmental understanding, as well as feeling, rests upon which metaphors control our attention and structure our debates.

Wilderness is an Experience

One of the most powerful metaphors with which an American conservation writer must work is that which identifies 'wilderness' with 'experience.' This seems contradictory in one fundamental way: 'wilderness' by definition denotes the untouched in nature, that land outside human activity and experience. Yet a force field in our culture draws people toward the edge of wilderness, into a dream that we can actually pass over the canyon's edge, or into the forest's gloom, and feel what is utterly beyond society. Once the land has been trampled on or 'experienced,' it ceases to be wild.

Conservationists from John Muir to Aldo Leopold have agonized over the need to popularize wild areas with urban dwellers. This was both to sustain political support for protection efforts, and for the psychological and spiritual health of crowded, overworked citizens. But as soon as such efforts succeed they threaten wildness with crowds, automobiles, snowmobiles, roads, and development. As Thoreau and Muir realized, the answer cannot be transportation of large numbers of people to celebrated wild sites. The wilderness idea was believed critical, yet it was potentially deadly to conservation. Instead of recommending mass visitations of wild areas, these writers sought to use descriptions of people-within-wilderness to suggest ways anyone could enjoy gardens, 'tame' woods, and parks.

Trying to model ordinary life on a tradition of wilderness adventure (including invasion and destruction) is a staple of advertising. Witness the constant television commercials for four-wheel-drive vehicles reaching dramatic cliff edges, or secluded rainforest waterfalls. The metaphor 'wilderness experience' has been a selling point for American identities since the earliest European investors wrote to lure their compatriots across the Atlantic.

From this interpretation of early American experience came the Development Ethic, which has proved a stronger determinant of world environmental history than the struggling Environmental Ethic. The outwardly expanding frontier in developmental space produced 'frontiersmen,' obsessed with growth and progress within themselves.

Expansion, whether in personal life, national politics,

12

or international commerce, is a compelling model for action. Conservation writers must confront it carefully, through creative strategies, rather than stand in its path. Even writing to reduce desire for commodities must be expressed in the language of the developer. The conservation writer must speak of expanded personal experience.

Nature is a Farm

In the 1880s many resources, from timber to buffalo, became scarce. The conservation movement, predecessor of today's environmental movement, began to take shape. The 1890 census announcement that the "frontier is now closed" had great symbolic impact on the nation. If the wilderness/ frontier model of resource use could no longer guide social action, what kind of revised model was necessary? By 1900 the human impact upon nature was becoming part of social debates concerning resources. Industry recognized its own effects upon reproductive stocks of some kinds, and attempted to determine the maximum yields which were sustainable for the long run. Gifford Pinchot, founder of scientific forestry in the United States, traveled to Europe to learn sustainable practices. The Progressive Era of Theodore Roosevelt and Pinchot celebrated science, efficiency, and rational planning. From this period came the powerful metaphor nature is a farm, with its implication that species can be harvested ad infinitum through scientific husbandry. The code phrase for this was "sustained yield," which passed into our commonsense vocabulary and still carries the weight of the obvious in resource discussions; it also laid the foundation for the ambiguous "sustainable development."

According to the sustained yield model, a stock's capacity to reproduce depends upon the number of breeding adults left alive in a given year. Productivity increases with effort (energy and capital) up to a point of maximum sustained yield (MSY), then declines as harvesting removes more offspring than seed stock can annually produce. "The

Progressives' idea was that government scientists would pinpoint each stock's MSY and present their findings to lawmakers, who would then limit the harvest to that level" (McEvoy 220).

This rested upon the false assumptions that (1) determinations of MSY would be made by impartial scientists; (2) impartial lawmakers would act on the scientific information to impose proper harvesting limits; (3) the law would command adequate obedience from resource industries; on the theoretical level (4) harvesting activities were treated as the single important variable in determining long-term stocks. Random fluctuations in climate, disease, and interdependent species populations went unrecognized, as did new, intensive harvesting technologies, and fluctuating market demand.

The approach worked well for resources which enjoyed stable conditions, i.e., where human harvesting was the only interfering factor. These included seals and oceanic groundfishes, such as plaice and halibut (220), and Progressivism seemed promising in forestry. But in California sardine fishing, 'scientific' and managerial limits stripped the stock of its buffer against ecological change, and in the 1940s the industry collapsed.

The problem was that in the Progressive Era little was known of the intricate interdependence of species — the "complexity of the land organism," in Aldo Leopold's words. The very idea of treating a single species as a 'stock,' separated from other species, was naive. And just as this model oversimplified the nature side of the human/natural interaction, it failed to cognize the complexity of human harvesting activities.

Today forest products industries, enacting the nature is a farm metaphor on a broad scale, speak in their ads of sustained yield; they show photographs of 'caring' foresters replanting seedlings after 'harvest,' and in the background one sees the orderly rows of a monocultured plantation.

While ecologists intend a precise, analytical meaning by "sustained yield," industry copyrighters trade this for warm emotional connotations of nature's unending bounty.

Despite its obsolescence at the level of theory, it is important to remember that environmental writers must constantly confront, and use, variations of the sustained yield theme. Its offspring, sustainable development, has become part of commonsense within public discourse.

The Commons Is A Tragedy

Resource managers who reacted to overharvesting in the name of sustained yield sought a solution in the realm of property control. Conceptually, either privatization or rigid government control of a resource base would do. But without one of these, went the new myth, chaotic market activities will degrade a resource base to oblivion.

In 1968 Garrett Hardin synthesized and popularized this approach in his essay, "The Tragedy of the Commons" (Hardin, 1243). Beginning with a tale of competing farmers sharing a common grazing area in the 1830s in Britain, Hardin describes in mathematical terms the precise advantage to each of adding yet another cow, even though this cow is one more than the range can eventually carry. The negative effects of this single animal are small at first, and are distributed over all the cows (which grow thinner), the grass (which begins to disappear), and the farmers (who grow poorer by invisible degrees). But the benefits are great, and accrue only to the aggressive individual with the new cow. Since every farmer will reach the same strategic conclusion, the grazing commons will finally be destroyed.

This metaphor, the commons is a tragedy, has become enormously influential in global resource discussions, especially concerning population problems. It is often alleged that, just as the farmers in the story lack community perspective, poor people of the world produce children for their own short-term gain, indifferent to gradual but relentless

15

environmental degradation. Hardin blames human nature and the solution he imagines is strong governmental control. In the case of overpopulation, he recommends that the rich of the world keep the poor out of their "lifeboats" by force (Hardin 1974).

Hardin's rhetorical move from an overgrazed common pasture to large-scale resource problems of a 'global commons' has been influential. Let us examine its seductive implicit structure.

Instead of focusing attention on the real problem with resource abuse — the actions of rich and powerful individuals and organizations — Hardin's treatment of the commons directs us into the depths of historical nostalgia. Beguiled by village green images of our own romantic history, and contemplating those extra cows munching the commons, we are horrified to picture such landscapes threatened by starving millions. The choice seems be between nature protected by cruel population policies, and a world overrun and degraded.

For Hardin, 'mutually agreed upon coercion' prevents the tragedy of the commons. In practice this means Third World populations are sometimes forced to use birth control. It is widely acknowledged now that this Hobbesian picture of 'universal human nature' as savage is really a reflection of actors in the market economy of capitalism. But 'pure' destructive market behavior is seldom found in individuals acting within their home communities. On the contrary, the great problem for almost everyone in the modern world is how to temper market behavior with the kinder mitigations of community life. Only corporations (and sometimes governments) exemplify the 'pure' stupidity of ultimate resource depletion for short-term profit. Of course individuals within corporations could make bizarre decisions, say to eliminate Old Growth forests, or all the whales, or all the water in the Ogalala Aquifer. These individuals hold terrible power over the rest of us. But their behavior stems from their institutional culture, not from human nature. There is an impending tragedy of the global commons, but the threat is from individuals running the huge organizational systems we humans have invented, especially those driven by the single goal of profit maximization.

In the following section I discuss a newer model of human/natural relations which seeks to include a more concrete concept of community. It appears quite promising on the policy and practical levels, but we shall find theoretical excesses in some articulations of its central metaphor.

Bioregions are Natural Visions

In recent years a number of writers have proposed metaphors which attempt to recognize greater complexity in the human/nature interaction. One of these, known as the Bioregional Vision, has caught on with many conservation writers.

Bioregionalism begins from the perception that human beings live, work and think effectively only within certain spatial limits; forests, farms, towns, parks, and cities can be planned with this in mind, or they can be left to unplanned sprawl and the effects of overbuilding and overpopulation. Bioregionalism asserts that such planning ought to begin with a biological region, such as a river valley, a coastal zone, or a mountain range. Boundaries of these regions will reflect 'natural' ecosystems, especially as they provide the basis for local economic life and human society.

But how long has it been since ecosystems provided the basis for local economies and social lives? Our society cultivates an idealized vision of tribal peoples living simply from a bounty of nature. But the truth is, even ancient peoples were involved in enormous trade networks (Wolff). Today these networks cross nearly all geographical boundaries. Modern people in industrial societies like the U.S. sip tea from India, drive cars from Japan, drink Colombian coffee, grill Canadian salmon. Our clothing is sewn in Asia and

17

Central America, our winter fruits are flown in daily from Chile, and our books may be printed in Italy.

Recently I stood on the Rhode Island shore and spoke with a fisherman about the thousands of small sharks he and his crew were netting each day. Their fins went to China, their fillets to the Caribbean, while their cartilage headed for health food stores in the U.S.A. So it goes with any local product of nature: lumber sails for Europe or Japan, fish fly on commercial jets from New York to the countries of the fished-out Mediterranean. Bears are poached in Maine and their gall bladders wind up in China; parrots, trapped in South America, are smuggled north to the pet shops of Los Angeles. The world is a crazy-quilt of markets and trade routes, superimposed over the mosaics of bioregional communities. Even tribal people in New Guinea wear Madonna T-shirts, drink Coke, and watch TV.

This, bioregionalists may quickly point out, is precisely the problem: political and economic boundaries don't mirror natural ones, but they should. And perhaps this is so — but notice that we have shifted onto normative ground. We have left the observation that bioregions, principally watersheds, are the foundation of all life (in the sense that every person, and every production process, can be located in some watershed), and we have begun to speak about how people ought to reform their ways of living (so that trade is mostly confined within watersheds).

Andrew Ross, in his book *The Chicago Gangster Theory of Life*, argues that popular culture today is rife with a species of fallacious argument he calls "biologism": reading off prescriptions for culture and society from biological relationships. Bioregionalism is just one example he discusses. How, exactly, does this fallacy occur?

One might begin by 'seeing' cooperation between individuals and between species as more fundamental than aggression and competition. If the animals are peaceful, should we be peaceful also? But what if we are wrong in our interpretation of nature?

If future ecologists should discover some 'more fundamental' sense in which animal competition structures animal society, would we be bound to change our own ways of living? That is, if the animals turn out to be warlike, should we be warlike? Of course not. We would simply maintain that our evolved morality is superior to that of nature. One can applaud bioregional metaphors, analogies and projections, and work to implement them while maintaining concern over the tone and argumentative strategy which 'reads off' society from nature.

The appeal of this metaphor for conservation writers lies its invocation of the natural world and its recognition of the rich social and spiritual values which enlightened humans seek within this realm. But the boundaries marking the *edges* of bioregions often turn out to be products of social decisions — projections of social/political needs, rather than the edges of watersheds, valleys or rainforests.

Conclusions

The metaphors discussed in this essay haunt American landscapes and the writers who shape them. As we have seen, each arose in response to particular experiences and served to conceptualize new solutions to environmental problems. In turn, each contained the seeds of new problems which eventually appeared. We have no choice but to keep trying to manage nature with the best models we can get, but we would be wise to study the culturally shaped metaphors which inspire model building.

Conservation writers need to freely invent new metaphors for the shifting crossroads of nature and culture, but they also need to critically examine each one. We need historical perspective on metaphors that seem to describe our human-landscape interactions, especially when they seem to offer moral guidance as well.

Three

John Muir writing 'God's Fine Wilderness'

Introduction

John Muir forged a new language for nature in America. As he crossed the bridge from the Christian faith of his childhood to the Darwinian science of his education, Muir adapted the rich language of the King James Bible to the needs of a secular ecological conscience. He made the transition at precisely the right moment for the conservation movement, and evolved a passionate idiom with which millions of readers could feel comfortable. I discuss some of the reasons his essays and books reached into the hearts of his generation, and show why his textual strategies still serve conservation writers well. But Muir didn't spring from a void. Later in this essay I discuss European writing traditions which provided him with issues, heroes, rhetorical models and even specific scenes for emulation. From a century's distance, we can see both the richness of his influences and the habitual blind spots which his heroes passed on.

Muir's Background and Achievements

John Muir (1838-1914) is regarded today as a founder of the conservation movement in America. Born in the coastal village of Dunbar, Scotland, in his early years he absorbed the wild ocean, the fierce winter winds, and the nearness of the fishermen to raw nature. With equal intensity Muir absorbed the strong, poetic language of the King James Bible, which would one day give him a base from which to develop an effective style of his own. He was beaten by his father every day if he had not memorized his assigned portion. By age eleven he could recite the entire New Testament, and portions of the Old, by heart. In that year his hard Cambellite Calvinist father moved the family to the rough Wisconsin frontier.

After the sixth grade his father kept him on the farm and turned him and his brothers into slaves behind the plow. Denied books, a morning fire, a rest for sickness, he followed the oxen down the furrows year after dreary year. His father read scripture and watched him from the study window. Frost on the clods of dirt, pain in stiff leather shoes, the red sun breaking over the trees, these became formative memories. In those days he watched brave chickadees for lessons of heart. Spiraling geese, wing to wing with their lifelong mates, offered lessons of love. John Muir walked his nine miles before noon, nine miles behind the plow with stringy 14-year-old arms and legs, but with his iron will.

Against his father's objections, Muir left for college as soon as he could — age 22. His professors at the University of Wisconsin recognized his extraordinary promise, and despite his lack of basics encouraged him to pursue science or medicine. Nurtured by these men and their wives, Muir learned a good deal of botany and other sciences before he left at the end of the year. He worked on his father's farm another season, then wandered in the Canadian wilderness considering his future. When he returned he still had no firm plan. Creative with tools and engineering, Muir went to work in factories, designing machines and managing men.

One day the tip of a file flicked into Muir's eye, dislodging the aqueous humor and blinding him. Soon the other eye darkened in sympathetic blindness. During the months he spent in a shaded room, slowly healing, Muir determined that the rest of his life would be spent among the things of God rather than the things of Man. He set off on a walking trip from Indianapolis to the Gulf of Mexico. This took months, and led him to a fresh view of nature; years later it became the basis for one of his books.

This fresh view involved an encounter with his first alligator. He was twenty-nine, standing in the still, sweltering Florida swamp, when he looked upon the unspeakable face of the creature with its alien smile. People called it devil-made, for God would not create so foul a beast. But the monstrous appearance pointed to a possibility more sinister than Satan. What if the gator was no exception, but Nature's rule? What if none of Earth's inhabitants were made for the human race? The alligator served himself, as anyone could see. But what of the Chickadee, and the Oak? What of the noble mountains — for whom were they made? *Not for Lord Man*, Muir wrote later on.

This discovery of Muir's could be interpreted as his personal rejection of Christianity, in which every aspect of 'the creation' was made for Adam, Eve, and all who followed. In that sense the discovery was a stubbornly independent moment in which Muir embraced a portion of the Darwinism toward which he already leaned.

Muir made his way to California, and wandered the Sierras for weeks at a time. He survived on acorns and a crust of bread, sometimes a bit of tea. Eventually he began to write essays, all of which were later published. Through this he gathered a large public for some successful preservation efforts. The message Americans had ignored from Thoreau just 40 years earlier, many were now ready to hear.

As John Thaxton has written:

> A one-man-band of a conservation movement, John Muir fell in love with Yosemite Valley and America fell in love with what he saw and felt there, and with how

powerfully he showed it. America fell in love with Muir because here was the real thing, the genuine crackpot holy man living in a prelapsarian wilderness, bonding with water ouzels and Douglas squirrels, remembering the glaciers, probably living on nothing but locusts and wild honey, firing out essays the public eagerly awaited. Sometimes he sounded like Saint Francis communing with the animals, at others like Jeremiah declaiming the nighness of the end (Muir viii).

Eventually Muir influenced President Theodore Roosevelt, who camped with him in Yosemite Valley, and who was in a position to preserve land. Muir appeared as an extreme 'preservationist,' which suggests "hands off nature" and alarms many people, rather than a negotiable 'conservationist,' with its associations of a mixture of human and wild interests. This radical stance was useful, because Muir provided a left-wing pole for the environmental debates of his time. Gifford Pinchot, first head of the Forest Service, was able to portray himself by contrast as a moderate. Muir despised Pinchot's policies, such as allowing sheep to graze and destroy meadows on federal land, but the two of them worked in a dialectical way for the benefit of long-term conservation. Pinchot succeeded in protecting vast tracts of land in National Forests under the banner of "mixed use." Without Muir's voice demanding purist measures Pinchot would have protected far less land (Lawrence and Garvey).

Muir eventually co-founded the Sierra Club, and bequeathed the spirit of his religious-sounding zeal to the 20th Century Green movement. But how, exactly, did Muir's writing awaken the nation?

Muir's Rhetoric and its Implied Subjects
In one of his most popular essays, "A Wind-Storm in

the Forest," we may observe some characteristic rhetorical moves. Muir has portrayed himself exploring a tributary of the Yuba River in December of 1874:

> The day was intensely pure, one of those incomparable bits of California winter, warm and balmy and full of white sparking sunshine, redolent of all the purest influences of the spring, and at the same time enlivened by one of the most bracing windstorms conceivable. ...I lost no time in pushing out in the woods to enjoy it. For on such occasions Nature has always something rare to show us...
>
> I heard trees falling for hours at the rate of one every two or three minutes... The gestures of the various trees made a delightful study. Young Sugar Pines, light and feathery as squirrel tails, were bowing almost to the ground; while the grand old patriarchs, whose massive boles had been tried in a hundred storms, waved solemnly above them... (Muir 154)

Muir attains the top of the highest ridge, then decides to climb a tree. He selects a 100 foot tall Douglas Spruce [Fir]:

> Being accustomed to climb trees in making botanical studies, I experienced no difficulty in reaching the top of this one, and never before did I enjoy so noble an exhilaration of motion. The slender tops fairly flapped and swished in the passionate torrent, bending and swirling backward and forward, round and round, tracing indescribable combinations of vertical and

horizontal curves, while I clung with muscles
firm braced, like a bobolink on a reed (156).

Muir's close observation of details is combined
with a self-portrait as field scientist, as when he wrote "the
gestures of various trees made a delightful study." His
religious background (and that of his readers) is brought
nearly to the surface with "...Nature has always something
rare to show us..."; there is usually the sense that God's
revelation lies within, not concealed behind, Nature, waiting
for humans to open their eyes. Poised between his father's
Cambellite Presbyterianism and Darwin's evolutionary
thinking, Muir seemed precariously faithful to both, using
the former vocabulary as a new and grand set of metaphors
for the latter. But to give a twist to a present-day distinction,
he only showed this, he never told his readers this is what he
was about.

In fact, his use of religious, even fundamentalist,
imagery for natural events was so ambiguous as to inspire
a range of interpretations. Steven Fox's *John Muir and his
Legacy: the American Conservation Movement*, the first
biography written after the Muir family released his private
journals and letters to scholars, revealed that Muir had
decisively rejected Christianity. So his use of rich biblical
language was indeed metaphorical — more so than his
readers believed. In this sense his language was like that of
many people in our own time who deny they are Christians,
yet invoke God's purpose in describing nature (Kempton,
Willet, et al.). Perhaps, like Muir, these people believe that
this is the only language they have to express their feeling
that nature is sacred.

His language created an ideal bridge for people raised
in the church and uneasy about the rising power of science.
Muir opened a way for people to put their spiritual feelings
into a new sort of relation with the natural world.

Muir manages to embody in his observer's position

26

the personae of scientist, preacher and cultured landscape critic. But there is more: by emphasizing his solitary and simple life, his crust of bread and cup of tea, his bed of rocky earth on cold nights beside a lonely fire, he adopts yet another persona, that of monk or ascetic. This figure abandons wife and children, warm home and good food, to embrace mountain winds and hard climbs, lightning storms, mountain lions and grizzlies. He watches and listens intensely for the secrets of nature. Muir's language embraces nature as cultural landscape, and projects without reservation his aesthetic preferences as if they were descriptive of objective facts.

Observing that a sheer cliff which remains in a mountain's shadow all day is smooth, while nearby sections exposed to sunlight are rough, he concludes that Yosemite Valley was formed by glaciers. This flew in the face of received academic wisdom, but he was right. In this case, as in many botanical discoveries, he seems to have the focus and interests of a field scientist.

But just as often he abandons the scientific voice and focus, and extols the healing effects of wildness for members of a sick, crowded, industrial society. Part of his genius was his ambiguity, his ability to switch observer's positions and appeal to the reader's interests and needs across a wide and undefined spectrum.

Muir's gentle persona, whether as scientist, preacher or aesthetic critic, brought all his intensity and determination, all his joy in physical exertion and emotional expression, to the very edge of nature and held it there, arrested and looking on as if through glass. His hands seemed never to touch or harm a single living thing. And the more essays he wrote, the more details of waving tree fields or bold grizzly bears in wildflower meadows he amassed, the more his audience came to see itself as gentle observers of nature as well. In this way he created the subjectivity of many city-bound readers, the implied subjects of his narrative adventures.

Wilderness preservation was not only for the benefit of forests, deserts and mountains; it was also for a rough, violent society that needed to see its gentle and spiritual side. Muir's success as a conservation writer exemplifies Richard Rorty's point that moral progress occurs when a writer's private obsession happens to meet a public need. Muir's texts seem lucid, transparent windows onto natural scenes of glory. Sometimes they resemble science, with its illusion of authorless writing, its clear lens on a theory and supporting facts at hand. (This is especially true in his early essays on glaciers.) But Muir the gentle soul is also a presence in every essay; he stands before nature filled with awe and appreciation; he does not hunt, nor build a remote cabin, nor cut down trees. He barely eats. From whence does his ferocious energy come? This is less important in a biographical than in a rhetorical sense. That is, what does the reader imagine the answer to be? Because whatever the springs of the reader's own energy in life, whatever the reader's values and interests, Muir's wilderness descriptions suggest that those civilized, cultured and complex interests can be brought right up to the very edge of nature without causing harm. "You too, dear reader," he seems to say, "might bring the hectic life inside your head to within inches of a living stream, or a storm-whipped pine." You might see as Muir has seen, might appreciate without destroying.

Thus we discover not only Muir's observer position within the text, or at the edge of every ecological frame, but also a potential position for ourselves. We, as Muir-like visitors to the wild, whether as unobtrusive observer scientists, religious seekers, or aesthetic consumers, are the implied subjects of his works. But not everyone can be included in this "we." Those acts of self-denial, like his living for weeks on a crust of bread and a bag of tea, contain a broad hint for all who might follow: Muir has achieved his revelations not by means of a social vision which could sustain families and communities, but through the denial of all that. His is the leave-taking of one single man. He walks through an invisible doorway into the mountains, and if we follow it will hurt.

Sacrifices are necessary: you must leave behind wife and home, warmth and food. This restriction selects wilderness experiences — with rare exceptions — for males only. As for the Indians, inhabitants and appreciators of the woods for thousands of years, "most of them are dead or civilized into useless innocence" (Muir 18-19). Thus the wilderness is further restricted to white males alone.

If we inquire about these white male travelers to the wilds, we soon realize they must possess an education. Without a certain kind of aesthetic training, Muir's judgments about the grandeur of viewscapes, about their sublime character, make no sense. Just as Thoreau learned when he entered the Maine woods and found pig farmers content with their sawed-off trunks, one must come from civilization to appreciate the trees. William James would later have a similar shock of realization in the backwoods of North Carolina, when he grasped that the ugliness of a muddy farm existed only for him, while the owners were blissfully proud. Conservationists sometimes imagine they favor all parts of nature equally, but like the readers they must persuade, writers favor certain views, and species, over others. If nature can be beautiful, then some of it can be ugly, and one's education matters.

Muir is after all a writer, and his fashioning of popular and politically galvanizing texts is a sophisticated affair. The more we interrogate his literary personae, and his implied subjects, the more remote the wildness he found seems to become. Ironically, the better we understand that invisible door through which he passed, the more clearly we see ourselves in Muir.

Despite lack of formal degrees Muir was beautifully educated — he had read many European classics and studied with scientists who taught him Darwin, Agassiz, and other leading thinkers; and Muir possessed a scathing critique of industrial cities grounded in his own factory work and months of blindness. No modern person, perhaps, was ever more heartsick at cities and so in need of the forest. Caught up in his loving and inspired writing, we long for his vistas and see our thoughts in his own. And yet how many of us can pay the same price?

He practically begged his readers to abandon their crowded and overheated lives, and come to the western reserve lands. In his time already 2,000 tourists each summer made the trip. They spent a few vacation days on horseback seeing the sights. He even guided some of the parties.

Almost a century later we have taken Muir's advice with a vengeance, but without his holy restraint. Yosemite is overrun with tourists, all wanting three squares and a warm bed, all burning fossil fuels to get there. Snowmobiles and motorbikes chase off the animals and devour the silence. Did no one listen? All these people rush in for a bit of renewal, lured perhaps by the sentimental videotape sold by the park service, then hurry back to their normal grinds. They bring a modicum of landscape education, perhaps a sort of mass acculturation of Muir's judgments, but they do not experience his wildness in their groups.

Has anyone developed a workable social ecology? Is there a vision of how sustainable communities can exist on the edge of wildness? These are burning questions for our time, for our future conservation writers. Muir did not solve them for us; instead he created a strong textual maze to lure us out from lives he rejected. He bids us follow him — alone and fit, celibate, and well read. As William Cronon has said, "Muir left out the poor, women, and the working classes" (Holt and Garvey). He left out anyone unable to make the climb.

Writers employ textual personae, and project images of implied subjects which tempt our readers toward action. Writers of advertising and political speeches spend day and night on this task. Muir redescribed ecosystems as something to admire and even revere. In doing this, he created an implied subject — the admirer — who was a redescribed American in the landscape. This figure was gentle and alert, distinct from the hunter, pioneer, farmer, and industrialist. Just how this person got education and sustenance, and just how his/her wilderness experience could be shared by hundreds of millions of others, was left for another generation to work out.

Writing in the Contact Zone

In her book, *Imperial Eyes: Travel Writing and Transculturation*, Mary Louise Pratt coins the useful term "contact zone" for those areas of the world usually described as "frontiers." When Europeans began to spread out across the globe 500 years ago, they conceptualized the lands they found as frontiers; but of course such places were only frontiers from the vantage point of Europe. From within, they were the inhabited landscapes of people who perceived the newcomers as invaders. Within these landscapes great struggles took place — and still do — over who will control territories, natural resources, and labor power. Such places, Pratt suggests, might be called "contact zones" to indicate the multiple viewpoints and peoples locked in ongoing struggle, resistance, and negotiation. The very word "frontier," to which we are so accustomed by popular culture, suggests two great European myths: the discovery of forests, animals, and other resources vast, plentiful, and essentially empty of human owners; and (somewhat contradictorily) humans of sub-European status who, though they might live in the frontier zones, and even claim the land there, don't really deserve it because they don't use it properly (in the European way).

American writers use and transform a rhetoric of nature forged by European explorers, scientists, and investors. Those earlier writers spoke of nature wild and plentiful, a challenge or a garden waiting only for colonial settlement and development to bring out its 'highest and best use.' The tribal peoples, now believed to number possibly 100 million in 1492, who inhabited landscapes of the Americas, were carefully erased from such pictures.

Styles of imperial imagination and textual representation developed in relation to Africa and other contact zones as well as the Americas. As we will see, textual strategies can be traced from Carl Linnaeus and his followers in the early 18th Century, through Mungo Park and other African explorers in the last half of that century, and then to Alexander von Humbolt in his vast writings on South America in the first half of the 19th Century. In this lineage we find Thoreau and Muir.

Just as one can learn from Muir and others how to represent nature as a pristine, wild garden, bearing divine or mystical secrets, offering refreshment and healing from a sick, industrial world, one can also learn to see what Muir left out.

One tradition which influenced Muir was European travel writing. It begins 500 years ago with the writings of Columbus, Vespucci, and others. Consider this passage from Columbus' 1493 letter to the king and queen of Spain:

> All these islands are very beautiful, and distinguished by a diversity of scenery; they are filled with a great variety of trees of immense height, and which I believe to retain their foliage in all seasons....There are besides in the same island of Juana seven or eight kinds of palm trees, which, like all the other trees, herbs, and fruits, considerably surpass ours in height and beauty. The pines also are very handsome, and there are very extensive fields and meadows, a variety of birds, different kinds of honey, and many

sorts of metals, but no iron (Pratt 126).

Mary Louise Pratt notes the trope of 'the erasure of the human' in this passage — the celebration of a 'found' nature ripe for European uses. She reminds us that Columbus followed this letter with a second one "proposing not his integration into the Edenic world he had found, but a vast project of colonization and enslavement to be presided over by himself." Explorers' letters and other writings typically brought the excitement of discovery to readers back home. Their works, like many 'nature' essays today, were organized according to the structure of a journey: leaving home, arriving, ordeals, the moment of revelation when a startling view appears (mountain, lake, forest, etc.), then the return home.

Never mind that these discoveries were of other peoples' homes, not to mention habitats of other species. And never mind that the ordeals leading up to revelations were usually mediated by native guides, often bent beneath the Europeans' equipment, sometimes carrying the explorers themselves.

In the text the journey appears much like that of a hero's quest in a folk tale. The young person leaves home, suffers ordeals, acquires native guides and friends, finally achieves a worthwhile prize (either of treasure or self-knowledge), then returns home with a new wisdom and maturity, to contribute his (sometimes her) discovery to an original small community. This pattern, discussed by Otto Rank, Carl Jung, Heinrich Zimmer, Joseph Campbell and others, achieved a particular purity within the mythology of many Native American tribes. Here the goal was for every young person to fast and experience solitude as part of a vision quest. In this moment the person met his or her guardian spirit, and received from this person a lifelong mission. One might become a war leader, a shaman, an expert with horses, a fine basket maker, and so on. The spirit usually appeared as an animal, whose form itself was a clue to the young seeker's future. I call this version "pure" because no material prize was at stake, just a commitment to serve one's community.

All of this entered western popular culture in a powerful way in George Lucas' *Star Wars* trilogy, for which Joseph Campbell served as a consultant. Later Bill Moyers' televised interviews with Campbell secured him and his Jungian views a wide audience and influence.

The tropes of quest-journey writing are powerful indeed in western society today, and it's no wonder so many nature writers make use of the form. In the many books and films that have poured from Hollywood in the past two decades with this structure, common features have been the innocence of the hero and the exotic nature of the lands he/she discovers. He may encounter good and evil characters there, but he never experiences himself as evil — as bringing imperialism, microbes, etc., to other people's homes. In fact, in popular culture, the hero's journey tale has merged with American frontier mythology, so that the endless leaving (from the civilized east) and adventuring (in the exotic west) is repeated again and again.

Eventually we must ask whether John Muir's Sierra landscapes, at the time he explored them, were 'empty' nature or someone else's home. But to return to our story of how nature writing evolved, let us skip 300 years from Columbus to the time of Alexander von Humboldt. This wealthy German, with his French partner Aime Bonpland, arrived in South America in 1799. They spent five years exploring the forests and mountains, then returned to Europe where Humboldt produced 30 books on his travels in 30 years. He was considered "the most creative explorer of his time," and the writer of "a model journey of exploration and a supreme geographical achievement" (111). From the *Beagle* Darwin would write that his "whole course of life is due to having read and re-read Humboldt's *Personal Narrative* as a youth."

Humboldt reimagined the Americas for Europe, re-presenting the new world in much the same way Columbus had three centuries earlier. In Humboldt's work the Americas once again appeared as a "wild and gigantic nature." Troublesome human subjects rarely appeared in his heroic frames.

Pratt says:

> So engulfed and miniaturized was the human in Humboldt's cosmic conception that narrative ceased to be a viable mode of representation for him. He deliberately avoided it. ... The "view" or tableau was the form Humboldt chose for his experiments in what he called "the esthetic mode of treating subjects of natural history." ....His [effort], in his Views [of Nature], was to fuse the specificity of science with the esthetics of the sublime. .... The result, in the words of one literary historian, "introduced into German literature an entirely new type of nature discourse" (120-121).

Humboldt employs an abstract persona, thoroughly European and male. Pratt calls attention in the following passage to "the interweaving of visual and emotive language with classificatory and technical language, and the deliberate orchestration of the reader's response":

> At the foot of the lofty granitic range which, in the early ages of our planet, resisted the irruption of the waters on the formation of the Caribbean Gulf, extends a vast and boundless plain. When the traveler turns from the Alpine valleys of Caracas, land the island-studded lake of Tacrigua, whose

waters reflect the forms of the neighboring nananas, — when he leaves the fields verdant with the light and tender green of the Tahitian sugar cane, or the somber shade of the cacao groves, — his eye rests in the south on Steppes, whose seeming elevations disappear in the distant horizon.

From the rich luxuriance of organic life the astonished traveler suddenly finds himself on the drear margin of a treeless waste.

Pratt comments:

Having produced his reader's desolation, Humboldt sets about alleviating it, filling the wasteland ("stretched before us, like the naked stony crust of some desolate planet") with dense and powerful meaning. Displaying his own brand of planetary consciousness, he compares the Venezuelan Llanos to the heaths of Northern Europe, the interior plains of Africa, the steppes of central Asia. Pages of analytical, often statistical, description ensue, but in a language that is also filled with drama, struggle, and a certain sensuality.

Humboldt attempts to display nature as product of the endless expansion and contraction of hidden forces. He wants to show "nature's ancient communion with the spiritual life of man." He speaks of "her greatness" and "her speaking...forcibly."

Occasionally Humboldt mentions that "a few Indian slaves froze to death." Though he was strongly anti-slavery in his politics, he nevertheless took advantage of the Spanish colonial empire and its help in "discovering" and "viewing" this wild South American nature. His work established the "standard metonymic representation" of the "new continent," and reduction of a complex, inhabited land to "pure nature" in the "iconic triad of mountain, plain, and jungle" (121).

In 1866 the young John Muir, a college dropout working in a factory, wrote to his mentor, Jeanne Carr, of his longing to travel through South America. "How intensely I desire to be a Humboldt!" (Fox 47). But soon afterward he suffered the injury to his eye that blinded him for months. After that period of reflection he decided on his thousand-mile walk from Indianapolis to the Gulf of Mexico in Florida. He said he would "take off on a grand Sabbath day three years long." Botanizing through the tropics after the fashion of Humboldt, he would pile up "a stock of wild beauty sufficient to lighten and brighten my after life in the shadows."

At the same time, Muir was attracted by a different model of explorer's prose. In 1797 a 25-year-old Scotsman named Mungo Park appeared on the west coast of Africa alone and destitute. Sent by a British trading association to seek out opportunities for business (not the slave trade) he had survived a year and a half exploring the Niger Basin, and was about to return to England and write one of the most successful travel books of his time. Here is a passage from his *Travels in the Interior of Africa*:

> My thirst was by this time become insufferable, my mouth was parched and inflamed; a sudden dimness would frequently come over my eyes, with other symptoms of fainting; and my horse being very much fatigued, I began seriously to apprehend that I should perish of thirst. To relieve the burning pain in my mouth and throat, I chewed the leaves of different shrubs, but found them all bitter and of no service (Pratt 49).

As a young boy, Muir had devoured this book, as he had Humboldt's *Personal Narrative of Travels in the Equinoctial Regions*.

By contrast with objectivist science writing, Pratt comments, Park's speaker is responsible and self-dramatizing. "The language of the emotions — consolation, repine, hopes, insufferable — assigns value to events." Park's most memorable scene "depicts his deepest moment of crisis, when, pillaged by bandits in hostile territory, he is left for dead in the desert." Finding himself "naked and alone, surrounded by savage animals, and men still more savage," Park confesses, "my spirits began to fail me." He is saved by a naturalist's epiphany:

> At this moment, painful as my reflections were, the extraordinary beauty of a small moss, in fructification, irresistibly caught my eye.... for though the whole plant was not larger than the top of one of my fingers, I could not contemplate the delicate conformation of its roots, leaves, and capsula, without admiration. Can that Being (thought I), who planted, watered, and brought to perfection, in this obscure part of the world, a thing which appears of so small importance, look with unconcern upon the situation and sufferings of creatures formed after his own image? — surely not! (77-78).

Let us pick up our travel-to-conservation story with Muir's biographer Frederick Turner:

> The natural manifestation of divinity conquered despair and brought resolution, the will to survive, and Park struggled onward to a small village where two shepard

guides took him to safety. ... The young man [Muir] who read it had already been rescued often enough from his own homely despair by various manifestations of nature and the force that lived through it, and he would not have missed the parallel (Turner 65).

A few years later Muir spent months in the Canadian wilderness. After the brutal childhood he had endured, it is perhaps not surprising that he chose this life to avoid the draft for the Union Army. In any case, as Turner relates:

He had been wading for days through streams, bogs, and swamps of ever greater difficulty when one morning he entered a huge tamarack swamp... Hours later, just when he seemed most weary and his feet numb with the icy waters of spring, he made a discovery. In a bed of yellow moss just above the surface of the swamp waters, he came upon Calypso borealis, the Hider of the North. No other plant was near it. The dense stand of tamarack crowded closes on all sides. One leaf and one small white bud reposed there on the moss bed like a welcome and a benediction. So unexpected was it, and so surpassing in its beauty here in the monochromatic swamp that Muir sat down beside it and wept (115-116).

Muir's epiphany reenacted Park's in the Niger Basin. The thousand-mile walk, and Muir's adventures in the mountains of California, reenacted Humboldt's travels and writings as well.

Many of Muir's textual strategies derive from traditions of travel writing, both the objectivist and the sentimental varieties. Next let us look at the American conservation movement as it existed before Muir arrived in the Sierras. Here too, we will find a rich tradition which shaped Muir's feelings and beliefs, and through which he perhaps shapes our own.

A Conservation Tradition

In *Landscape and Memory*, Simon Schama takes us back to the moment in 1852, in the foothills of the western Sierra Nevada, when a "scrambling, violent crowd of Italians, Chinese, Mexicans, and Germans," failed and soured '49ers, inhabited shacks and tents in the Mariposa. They worked as hunters, loggers, ditchdiggers, cooks, and whores, and their lives were only a little more stable that those of the Ahwahneechee Indians of Yosemite Valley, whom the whites soon destroyed (Schama 186).

One spring morning a hunter for one of the camps was tracking a wounded grizzly through the woods of sugar pine and ponderosa when he "came face to face with a monster. It was maybe fifty feet round and, close as he could guess, near three hundred feet high. It was a tree."

No one believed him until he showed them. This was a member of the species which came to be called *Sequoia gigantea*. In 1854 another ex-miner, George Gale, picked out the largest specimen he could find, 90 feet around the base and known as the Mother of the Forest. He stripped the tree of its bark to a height of 116 feet and shipped the pieces east, where they were stitched back together and displayed as a botanical marvel. The public in New York refused to believe this was not a hoax, and Gale went broke; but botanists were another matter. Asa Gray, the founder of Harvard's botanical garden, and his New York colleague John Turrell, named them and thus rescued the tree from being named after an English military hero by an English botanist. "The big trees were thus seen as the botanical correlate of America's heroic nationalism at a time when the Republic was suffering its most divisive crisis since the Revolution" (187). Schama explains that nationalist and religious rhetoric combined to exalt the trees: "The phenomenal size of the sequoias proclaimed a manifest destiny that had been primordially planted; something which altogether dwarfed the timetables of conventional European and even classical history." When it took five men three weeks to fell a single tree, James Mason Hutchings would declare "it was a sacrilegious act" (188).

In 1860 the Boston Unitarian and orator Thomas Starr King arrived in San Francisco to found a church. He proclaimed, "this purity of nature is part of the revelation to us of the sanctity of God. It is his character that is hinted at in the cleanness of the lake [Tahoe] and its haste to reject all taint." The Big Trees, Schama concludes, "...were sacred: America's own natural temple." The pious notion that they were contemporaries of Christ became a standard refrain: "...Muir counted the rings on one martyr to the axe and discovered that "this tree was in its prime, swaying in the Sierra winds when Christ walked the earth." This immense botanical mystery was part of what Muir called the "Holy of Holies" in Yosemite (190).

And this discovery of a sacred California valley, exemplifying an American essence, offered atonement for many past and present sins. The Big Trees were painted by Albert Bierstadt and others, and their protection was promoted by geologist Josiah Whitney and landscape architect Fredrich Law Olmsted. Finally the sacred/national feeling reached congress and the president.

On July 1, 1864, Abraham Lincoln, in the midst of the Civil War, signed an unprecedented bill that granted Yosemite Valley and its Big Trees to the state of California. At this point John Muir was 26 years old, and hadn't yet seen California!

Not only was Muir stirred by European travel writers, but by American events too. In later years he declared Thoreau his favorite author, and after Muir's death his copies of the collected works of Thoreau were discovered heavily annotated. As a rustic model, Muir may have admired Galen Clark, appointed "guardian" of the Mariposa Grove in 1864. From a distance (looking perhaps at a photograph of long-bearded Clark beneath a sequoia), one might take him for John Muir as the latter appeared thirty years later. So in personal style, including dress and hair, and in the mythical image of a 'cultured but wild man of the forest,' Muir had a distinguished predecessor.

If one accepts Mary Louise Pratt's argument that classical travel writing was the work of 'imperial eyes' reporting expansionist opportunities to European audiences, and further, if one grants that Muir's work stands within this tradition, then the question arises: How is he different? And partly this is to ask, is the American conservation movement itself different? Or is it just a variation on the theme of expropriation of exotic lands 'at the margin' for powerful interests 'at the center'? After all, as Rodrick Nash points out in *Wilderness and the American Mind,* there are many ways to consume nature. It is possible to rope off a 'natural area' for aesthetic consumption by distant urban elites; and this roping off may displace native inhabitants or 'obnoxious' species as surely as outright seizure for agriculture, mining, or forest clearance. Let us turn to the question, then, of the relation of conservation to imperialism.

Imperial Conservation?

Although today we associate environmentalism with left/liberal politics, for example with the Democratic Party in the USA, and with the German Greens, it hasn't always been so. In ancient China and in medieval Europe, monarchs protected forests and animals while nearby villagers starved; poachers on these lands were punished by torture and death.

One could study the Norman invasion of England in 1066, when William the Conqueror emptied villages and decreed blindness for anyone killing a deer. And everyone knows the Robin Hood legends reflect, however romantically, competition between landowners and peasants for 'the king's deer.' Schama writes of the Nazi occupation during World War II of the great Polish forest:

> Two ideas of the primeval forest were at war in occupied Bialowieza. The goal of the German terror, once Jews had been eliminated from the scenery, was to use violence (mauling by retrained hunting hounds became a routine punishment) to dissuade the local population from taking to the woods as partisans or aiding and abetting those who might already be there. ... Once its humans had been made docile, the forest could be prepared by dependable German foresters for its proper role as the Greater Reich's most splendid hunting ground. With its Polish-Lithuanian identity completely wiped out, it could be presented as a great, living laboratory of purely Teutonic species: eagles, elk, and wolves (71).

The key to travel writing in all the Europeans' 'new worlds' was the presentation of landscape without its indigenous owners. Only after these 'empty' lands were designated as "frontier," then 'cleansed' of natives by soldiers and settlers, could conservation in the modern sense arise. The United States difference was that after the Indians were gone, whites discovered a new problem: protecting nature from other whites. The enemy became not exotic others out ahead of the frontier, but rich industrial others coming up fast behind. This historical and political difference seems to mark off John Muir's career from the travel and conservation writers who preceded him. After all, weren't the problems he faced different? Weren't the natives already gone, and the threats to nature generated by industrial greed? Let us examine this question carefully. Just how close to the bloody frontier was Muir's experience?

The Muir family moved to the Wisconsin frontier in 1849. Weary and forlorn bands of Winnebago Indians came by begging for food, and one of them stole John's favorite horse. Later he learned they had treated it cruelly. Although prejudice and suspicion were kindled early, the day would come years later when he would take a wider view. In *The Story of My Boyhood and Youth*, he wrote:

> I remember my father's discussing with a Scotch neighbor, a Mr. George Mair, the Indian question as to the rightful ownership of the soil. Mr. Mair remarked one day that it was pitiful to see how the unfortunate Indians, children of Nature living on the natural products of the soil, hunting, fishing, and even cultivating small cornfields on the most fertile spots, were now being robbed of their lands and pushed relentlessly back into narrower and narrower limits by alien races who were cutting off their means of livelihood. Father replied that surely it could never have been the intention of God to allow Indians to rove and hunt over so fertile a country and hold it forever in unproductive wildness, while Scotch and Irish and English farmers could put it to so much better use (Fleck 35-36).

Mr. Mair pointed out that many of the white farmers were ignorant of proper farming methods, and asked how they would like to be pushed out by a newer group of real farming experts. John thought that Mr. Mair had the better side of the argument, and he glimpsed the fact that Europeans were using force to take what they wanted. Despite such insights, however, Muir would describe the Winnebagos as "blackmailing," "pig killing," and "cruel." Later he used such negatives as "dirty," "lazy," and "wife-stealing" to describe the Digger Indians of California.

Around 1852 the Ahwaneechees were driven from Yosemite Valley, where Muir arrived in 1868 at the age of 30. What were Muir's feelings about the 'cleansing' which had so recently made available the landscape with which he fell in love? In later years he would incorporate in *The Mountains of California* Chief Tenaya's sad, powerful speech which he made upon his people's final expulsion from the valley. But the elegy for vanished people is a familiar trope in American literature; perhaps it soothes the conscience after the deeds are done. Throughout Muir's life he was ambivalent about Indians. In *My First Summer in the Sierra* he wrote: "Perhaps if I knew them better, I should like them better. The worst thing about them is their uncleanliness" (Fleck 40).

In 1878, Muir joined a U.S. Coast and Geodetic Survey to go to the wild country of the Nevada-Utah border, country of the enemy of the Digger Indians, the Paiutes. This was the year of Indian unrest and wars in Idaho to the north of the survey party. Muir wrote to his future mother-in-law:

> If an explorer of God's fine wilderness should wait until every danger be removed, then he would wait until the sun set. The war country lies to the north of our line of work, some two or three hundred miles. Some of the Pah Utes [sic] have gone north to join the Bannocks, and those left behind are not to be trusted, but we shall be well armed, and they will not dare to attack a party like ours unless they mean to declare war, however gladly they might seize the opportunity of killing a

lonely and unknown explorer. In any case we
will never be more than two hundred miles
from the railroad (41).

Muir's focus was always 'God's fine wilderness,' and
in this passage we see how he relished the explorer's role
— Humboldt and Park achieved at last. The Indians with
their "uncleanliness" and "untrustworthy" ways seem to him
unworthy of occupying the grand landscapes Muir wishes to
preserve. In fact, he contrasts the risks of his journey with
"waiting until every danger be removed."

Does he count himself among white Californians
able to enjoy Yosemite and other sites *because* the natives
have been removed? Despite his broader perspective at
times, and his occasional journal entries about individual
Indians he admired, Muir seems for the most part a man of
his times on this issue. He arrived just after most (but not
all) of the Indian wars, and was eager to frame the land in
the language of botanist, wilderness preacher, and cultured
aesthete. He embraced the pre-existing rhetoric of sacred and
patriotic wilderness, and focused his considerable energies
on protecting the mountains from the industrial and touristic
hordes to come.

Perhaps, then, Muir is very much a travel writer of the
older European sort, at least in his separation of 'discovered'
landscapes from the people who live or recently lived there.
But what about his position within American conservation,
poised not against natives but against the greedy whites
coming up behind? And how different is this form of
conservation initiative from those of the imperial tradition?
Schama shows in detail that similar struggles over the proper
uses of a nation's forests, with 'folk' interests identifying
national resources with preservation, and 'crown' or
'government' interests wishing to exploit them, have played
themselves out in Germany, England and other countries. He
describes the battles between Muir and Pinchot as not much

different from those internal to various countries (and their cultures and ethnic groups) over the past 500 years.

The bitter arguments between John Muir and Gifford Pinchot over the fate of American forests at the beginning of the Twentieth Century and the continuing debate in the Pacific Northwest over the meaning of 'sustainable resources' in the forest, are only the latest edition of debates that have been continuing for five centuries (Schama 154).

Perhaps so. But if contemporary readers discover this great historical battle through John Muir's prose, so much the better. Muir embraced traditions of writing, conservation politics, and personal style, and carried them to impressive heights. He wrote lasting books, achieved real preservation victories, and is remembered as "John O' the Mountains," the wild yet cultured man.

Our task involves far more, however, than emulation or critique. We need to recognize the implied subjects in Muir's prose, and confront the limits of his vision and viewpoint. We need to incorporate Muir's writing as part of our own tradition, but find fresh ways to metaphorically redescribe our world. He spoke and wrote of "God's fine wilderness" at the moment when his fellow citizens needed the phrase and the sentiment. Though he didn't believe it literally, he metaphorically conveyed a genuine spirituality which we can feel today.

His issues, heroes, textual strategies, tropes and even set pieces were drawn from the traditions of imperial travel writing, yet in making the turn to look over his shoulder at his own people, and using his gifts to reform his nation, he drew battle-lines with which we can only agree. Our heroes shouldn't have to be perfect. That the social dimension of conscience is better addressed by others, using different rhetorical strategies, does not diminish his greatness. John Muir's enduring legacy for conservation writers is the magic of his gentle authorial persona, and its subtle power to encourage an ecological conscience like his own.

Four

Science Journalism Basics:
A Woodcock Singing Ground

Most persuasive writing is organized in three parts: first, the writer mentions values shared with readers in an effort to create a bond with them; second, the writer offers new information, something important but previously unknown to readers; third, the writer suggests an action the reader needs to take. The whole piece presents an argument like this: We agree on these principles; here are new facts; in order to apply shared principles to these new facts, you should act as follows. The action might be a vote, or a private effort like recycling; it might be private and negative, such as, don't cut down those old growth trees, or don't shoot those birds.

This persuasive structure is found in many genres: political speeches, op/ed columns, and environmental journalism. It may be blatant and direct, as in election appeals, or subtle and suggestive, as in nature essays or complex journalism. In these latter forms, the recommended action may be to rethink one's attitudes toward an ecosystem or species. The writer may hope to initiate a conservation process by calling attention to under-appreciated creatures or landscapes, or to newly-threatened ones, and the specific recommendation might be an implied "discuss this with your friends and neighbors."

Those who study rhetoric point out that arguments for action arise in response to crisis situations; the writer becomes aware of a valued resource under threat, and tries to change the course of events by sharing information. But there is room within this work for a wide variety of approaches. Nature poets like Mary Oliver and Pattiann Rogers call our attention to living things through the intensity and beauty of their poems; these are what Oliver has called "invitational" rather than "cautionary." Simply by absorbing them and responding emotionally, we are changed into people who wish to preserve the living things described. On the other hand, if a dam is about to rise, or a forest about to fall, or a roadless area about to lose protection, many writers will make direct and even shrill appeals for immediate action, such as calls to congress. Both kinds of conservation writing are important, even necessary, and a writer needn't choose. Take the path that suits your temperament and skills.

I want to discuss how I employed this three-part persuasive structure in the short article below, which concerns woodcock conservation. This was published in the newsletter of a land trust.

The first step was to establish a bond of common values with my readers. This wouldn't be difficult, because I live in a small town and I knew many of the organization's members. They already cared about protection of the wild, and were especially interested in looking after local ecosystems. However, not all of them were familiar with the woodcock, a shy migratory bird. How could I interest them in this particular creature? How could I present scientifically valid information about the significance of local landscapes for a migratory creature?

First, the editors and I ran a title above the piece saying Science Journalism. Then we ran a banner below this to signal that this was one article in a series: Bioregional

50

Perspectives on Little Compton Landscapes. By creating this series, we hoped to raise consciousness of our readers that we live in a particular kind of place, with very specific biological treasures, which we can enjoy and protect.

I will number the paragraphs in the order they appeared, and discuss each one.

I. It is an interesting challenge to investigate the significance of Little Compton landscapes for various species. Conservation work requires us to think regionally, in terms of watersheds and larger areas, but how do we get scientifically valid information about the role of local places in the fate of a population or a whole species? For this article I sought to learn about our habitat for birds in general, and for the American woodcock in particular.

Comment: I presented my readers with puzzles: How do we think regionally? How connect local with wider landscapes? How research the woodcock? I knew my readers would think of these questions eventually, and rather than set myself up as the expert, I drew them into the search for answers. This would be a mystery story, and we would share its investigation.

II. The website of Partners in Flight presents a rich overview of the birds' situation. That organization highlights the urgency of our bird conservation responsibilities. Between 1600 and 1900, 75 species of U.S. birds and mammals became extinct; 75 more disappeared between 1900 and 1980. Current rates are roughly two per year, and some ornithologists estimate many songbird species are vanishing at 1% annually. Surveys of woodcock breeding areas or 'singing grounds' indicate 2% annual losses recently (1985-95), and 2.4% annual losses longer term (1968-94).

Comment: This opens with a mention of "our bird conservation responsibilities." Would all people feel this? Should I spend time arguing for it? For a broader audience, I wouldn't assume this common bond, but rather proceed right into statistics. But I felt this audience would enjoy both the ethical perspective and the way woodcocks fit in.

III. The woodcock, a plump quail-sized creature with mottled black, brown, buff and gray feathers, round eyes and a long spear of a bill, is my favorite bird. It's famous for its late winter and early spring flight displays. The males fly higher and higher over the breeding grounds, making a twittering sound. When they reach 200-300 feet they become silent for a moment, then plummet with a melodic cry in a zig-zag to land suddenly and give a call which most people describe as a 'peent,' but which sounds to me like a burst on a kazoo.

Because it probes for earthworms with its long bill, it needs dense, second-growth wet woods, which Little Compton provides in abundance. This past spring our air was lively with woodcocks, flying at dusk and dawn, and sometimes late into the night with a full moon. Maps at the U.S. Geological Survey website (USGS/gov) display results of a recent count by the annual Breeding Bird Survey. They reveal that woodcocks are shorebirds. Little Compton appears in a thin black line, indicating relatively high numbers, down the Atlantic coast.

Comment: This would be a good opening, if I had been writing for a broad audience that might not like claims about shared environmental responsibilities. Here the bird becomes 'real' through sensory descriptions of its color and shape, its flight patterns, and its weird calls. There are images of things one would like to see: "the air was lively with woodcocks, flying at dusk and dawn, and sometimes late into the night with a full moon." This paragraph is invitational. The following one is cautionary.

IV. Woodcocks are disappearing. While hunters kill 1.1 million annually, the main threat appears to be habitat loss. In one West Virginia study, 127 woodcock sites were observed in the mid 70s and again in the mid 90s. Only 15% of the sites were still good habitat. 41% had become mature forest, 24% open fields or pastures, and 9% human developments. Multiply this pattern over the entire range of the Woodcock, and you see why every acre counts.

Comment: The second sentence seems to implicate hunters, but quickly moves to habitat loss as the culprit, and shows how this works. In other words, we have met the enemy, and he is us. The hunting issue is complex, and could be the subject of another article. But in terms of numbers of birds lost each year, the main problem is changing land use patterns. Now I move to two concluding paragraphs.

V. Living in pictorial landscapes as we do in Little Compton, we may not grasp the speed of land clearances across our region, and their effect on songbirds. When we consider bulldozing another lot for a project, it may seem a small loss in habitat. And this may be true for many species, such as deer, coyotes, crows, woodchucks and foxes. These creatures thrive in human-style landscapes, with fields and edges. But birds are another matter. Every patch of dense wet second-growth woods is precious to woodcocks. And an acre saved for them matters a great deal in the big picture.

VI. In this case the biological region, or bioregion, includes the East Coast and Mississippi River Flyways, and to a lesser degree much of the Northeast and the Southeast. Woodcocks are a mostly invisible treasure living among us, shyly displaying their strange ways. Everyone who seeks to understand their ecology shares a great intellectual task. Everyone who protects a green patch for them joins an aesthetic and ethical movement as well. Such a person is entitled to refer to that patch as "my Woodcock singing ground."

Comment: Knowing my audience for this piece to contain many people who have control over at least a few acres of coastal wetland, my appeal is for private action from them. They should takes steps toward long-term protection for their land, if possible, and at least refrain from developing — destroying, from the woodcock point of view — their plots in the near term. Finally, I invent an award and offer it to those who care: they are "entitled to refer to [the patch they protect] as "my woodcock singing ground." Who knows whether this idea could catch on? It at least suggests community pride and personal woodcock connection, through the modest path of keeping a single acre wet and green.

Five

Creative Nonfiction: Sharing Sacred Ground

I grew up in a Southern family in the 1940s and '50s, in a family that loved land and landscape, timber and animals. My father was a conservationist sawmill manager — how odd those joined words sound now — who established the first tree farm in our county. He taught me to despise clear-cutting, to love the animals we hunted, and to see the forest as a place for spiritual visits.

Above all, by example, the forest was a place to share with your children. But I struggled over how to do that with my youngest child, Eva. We lived far from the family woods, and she refused to go down with me during hunting seasons, the fall and winter months I love most.

In the early mornings when she was six and seven, she used to walk the edges of our back garden in Rhode Island. Wearing a big hat, she'd check every bush and berry and bird. She had a natural joy in being outside. And from those early days I had offered to take her hunting, or just to visit the woods when I went, but she'd shake her head before I could finish.

Eva was quite firm about avoiding the hunt. By the time I was fifty-five and she thirteen, I simply wanted her to see the woods. In the fall she was always busy with school

— Thanksgiving would cut into family plans; and over Christmas break, the ideal time, there were armed men in the forest.

"No, Dad."

"But it's safe. All my friends are careful. Hardly anybody would be down there."

"No, Dad."

Eva is quick. Her dark blue-green eyes sparkle, and she can say no with a disarming smile.

I kept offering fall and winter, but last winter she was sixteen and I finally faced facts: She wasn't going with me in those seasons. Soon she'd be gone.

Summer vacation wouldn't work, either, because the woods were transformed into a blazing hot rain forest complete with poisonous snakes and clouds of mosquitoes and redbugs — and even the odd gator.

That left only spring as a possibility. But I'd never liked chilly, wet March the same way, or felt it represented the woods as they appear in my memories. The floods come, the wildflowers rise, and the low places stand under water. Spring doesn't hold the majesty of the brisk fall, when bucks wear antlers and the yellow leaves crinkle underfoot and you can see through the oaks a long way. Spring is marshy and green, the air alive with singing and stinging insects, bass bullfrogs and treble peepers. Crows and hawks scream about mates and nests and feeding their fledglings. I felt a rush of panic as I thought about her growing up without ever seeing the Three-Buck Woods, the most beautiful part of our family forest, sacred ground where my father and I shared many adventures. Eva seemed to sense how important this was to me, and finally she agreed to go.

In Mississippi, my mother showed us the latest tornado damage in town and I ritually ate barbeque. Next morning, we stretched on rubber knee boots, armed ourselves with a camera, and set off down the river road.

As we hugged the gravelly curves, I pointed out tea-colored sloughs with their elegant trees — black gums and tupelos and cypresses, swollen at their bases and doubled in reflection. Every bend in the road had a story — "I shot a gobbler here, and he sailed out over there" — and Eva nodded patiently. I called on myself not to overdo it. I wanted her to catch the feeling of the place rather than listen to me, which she could do in our own kitchen.

We parked by the gate of our friend Doctor Jack, who owns the land on two sides, and started our walk. We came to a long row of aromatic cedars smashed by a tornado, their faded red wood splintered open, their tops still green as they lay in the sand.

Soon we reached the creek bordering our property, and listened to it roar through the culvert beneath the logging road. We turned right and walked up our east line until we came to the meandering cat slough. Here I had once watched a mother bobcat and two cubs from a nearby tree.

"If we want to reach the Three-Buck, we'll have to wade," I explained to her.

"OK." She smiled and brightened at the challenge. Barefoot, trousers rolled up, we eased into the muddy water. Squishing our way beside cypress knees, a mighty-wing spanned great blue heron flew out from behind a black gum tree. We walked slowly and I began to whisper. It always seems a holy moment when I approach this place.

Our land has been in the family for more than fifty years, and for me its heart is the Three-Buck Woods — forty acres of oaks and cypresses surrounded by longleaf pines. Here the trees are oldest and tallest, the vistas longest. The rich acorn crop brings deer, turkeys, squirrels, and songbirds together in abundance. Especially grand are the overcup white oaks, whose sweet acorns the animals eat first.

When I was nine my father dropped me off at the gate with a rifle and left me to wander for a whole day around a four-mile trail. Back then the woods felt dangerous, inhabited by fierce animals — boars and bobcats and panthers —

before forestry and wildlife biology had penetrated either the woods or me. An Old Testament sense of the wilderness was my guide, and I was drawn mysteriously toward the shadows of big trees. I expected to see a shaggy boar with curling tusks, or to feel the presence of God as He'd appeared to Abraham.

Growing up, taking on layers of knowledge, each with its own weight, felt like a dialogue with this forest. After the final visit here with my dad, fifteen years before, I had written: The Three-Buck Woods grows in such quiet / cypress, shagbark, oak, persimmon / mallards feed beneath the trees / my father and his woods are one.

Eva and I crossed a sage field and entered an opening in the oaks. Sometimes I've slipped up on deer or turkeys feeding here, but that day the whole thing was flooded. Wet since winter, the acorn flat of the woods lay beneath a foot of water. It was a grand sight, with the trees open and the air still.

"This is where it happened," I said. She knew I was talking about how the Three-Buck got its name. Back in the mists of time, on a crisp fall afternoon in the '60s, I'd heard the five quick shots from the distinctive rifle of my boyhood friend, Dennis. When the five of us who were hunting that day met at my truck, I looked into the back by the light of sundown and was astonished to find three big bucks. It was excessive even then, and each member of my circle carries the memory with a mixture of man-guilt and boy-pride.

Eva studied the flooded trees. She's told me she doesn't understand the hunting part of my legacy, despite all my words about friendship and tradition and the joys of cooking venison. Killing is repugnant to Eva, a vegetarian who protects mice in the kitchen. From her point of view, hunting is about needless killing, and therefore makes no sense.

Not long ago she said, "You know what's really disgusting? It's that — what do you call it — when you just

58

catch the fish and let it go?"

"Catch and release."

"Yeah," she laughed sarcastically, "Catch and release. You don't eat the fish, you just puncture it and let it go."

I agreed with her. Suddenly this practice, which people think morally superior to other kinds of fishing, seemed cruel.

"You let it go wounded and confused," she said.

"Enjoy pulling it in, feeling its desperation." I said.

"Making it bleed," she added.

"Yeah, introduce bacteria into the wound, put it in shock, and then 'release' it. What a word!"

"Catch a fish if you want to eat a fish," she said. "But don't torture a fish."

"And then feel righteous."

"Exactly. Just like dolphin-free tuna."

"What?" I asked, confused.

"Why not tuna-free dolphin? Why is it OK to kill one species but not the other?"

"I guess people think more of dolphins."

"Sea World, that's why," she says. "On TV."

Unlike factory farming, which can subject animals to cruel conditions — chickens kept standing on slanted wire surfaces, confined and unable to move, their beaks and toes cut off — hunting is about a single animal and about the hunter, who should bring great respect for it, as I believe and as indigenous hunting peoples often expressed. Native American hunters believed the animal's spirit understands the sacrifice of its life and body, and when an animal appears to a hunter it's the "give away." I've studied and written about this philosophy in the Creek and Mikasuki tribes, whose traditions hold that the animal sacrifices its life for a balance between humans and animals. A good hunter takes no more than is needed for food or medicine. The master spirit of the species, like the spirit of the individual animal, gladly gives up a single life. Thus a balance in living, an

59

ecology, is achieved and given a spiritual framework.

We stood listening to tree frogs and cicadas. This was the moment I'd wanted for years. My grandfather had ridden his horse in this timber in 1935, and seen great cypress trees standing in acres of purple violets. He'd negotiated for the timber with a man who kept a bear on a chain. My father bought the land in 1950, and cut the timber only once, lightly. The trees and wood ducks and butterflies, in the privacy of shadows and silence, were what he'd wanted to pass along to us.

Eva watched the woods the way I do, peaceful and alert. A pair of ducks flew near us, threading the trees in flashing colors, shrieking and then splashing down to swim. She smiled with pleasure.

As we made our way out, we noticed a red-tailed hawk and tracks of raccoons and possums. Back at the culvert a cottonmouth moccasin lay with its head inside a hole. Eva crept up and took its picture.

We stood for a while by the flooded creek in the last of the afternoon, with the low bright sun doubled in the water. The place was rich and green and alive with reflections.

The next day we took another approach to the land. We drove to within a mile of my woods, and walked in along the railroad tracks. The bed is high above the swamp, with wonderful views, and I'm always on the lookout for the shells of turtles up here. We found one, bell-shaped and weathered white, and I told her my theory that bobcats bring them up to sit and eat. Bobcats — or foxes, or coyotes. In a few minutes she spotted a live one, a box turtle with delicate red stripes down its neck. Though it tried to swim in a puddle and crawl, its head remained jammed against a long steel rail. "Let's rescue it," she said. I nodded and picked it up, carried it down to a grassy pool for release.

"So," she said, "maybe they come up here themselves and get stuck."

I nodded.

Eva and I didn't have to convince each other of anything. We didn't have to resolve our views about food and righteousness. But I needed to bring her to my woods, ritual site, and to stand there as she witnessed it.

Six

Five Kinds of Environmental Writing

For years I taught an advanced composition workshop in Nature, Landscape and Environmental Writing to African American, Native American, Hispanic and Portuguese students. During and after the course, they found ways to integrate personal environmental concerns within a wide range of career writing projects.

I will discuss several kinds of environmental writing. These include the environmental autobiography, the landscape history, the nature essay, and the environmental perception study. Finally I will illustrate the use of environmental writing in the master's thesis. Development of this course began with the National Rural Fellows program at the University of Massachusetts Amherst. My students were mid-career minority professionals, earning master's degrees in Regional Planning. After two years in that program I continued to develop a variety of undergraduate and graduate courses at the University of Massachusetts Dartmouth. My students here are of diverse backgrounds, including Portuguese, Cape Verdian, Native American, African American, French Canadian, Lebanese and Irish.

The Environmental Autobiography

This assignment is the cornerstone of my approach. It

invites students to think and write about how the environment of their childhood, including the physical as well as the cultural landscape, has made them the unique individuals they have become. How might they be different if they had grown up elsewhere?

This can be a daunting question, and I have found the following structure helpful:

A ------------------------ B

where point A represents a significant childhood event, and point B represents a poignant moment in adulthood, which has been deeply influenced by point A. Older students often have a rich integration of their life stages to work with for this assignment, but undergraduates around 20 years of age frequently appreciate the simplification of this structure, in order to focus on the role of environment in the formation of selfhood.

This helps students think through one of the great illusions of our culture, the idea that we are autonomous souls or minds, free of the environment. As anthropologist Richard A. Shweder has put it:

> By contrast [with the Oriyas of India], in the West, as Louis Dumont (1970) notes, each person is conceived of as "a particular incarnation of abstract humanity" (p.5), a monadic replica of general humanity. A kind of sacred personalized self is developed and the individual qua individual is seen as inviolate, a supreme value in and of itself. The self becomes an object of interest per se. Free to undertake projects of personal expression — personal narratives, autobiographies, diaries, mirrors, separate rooms, early separation from

bed, body, and breast, of mother, personal space — the autonomous individual imagines the incredible, that he or she lives in an inviolate region (the extended boundaries of the self) where he or she is free to choose (see Friedman and Friedman 1980 for the purest articulation of this incredible belief), where what he does is his own business (151).

A particularly fine model of writing which does not detatch but rather situates the writer within a particular time and place is the novel *Eva Luna*, by Isabel Allende. Here is the opening:

My name is Eva, which means "life," according to a book of names my mother consulted. I was born in the back room of a shadowy house, and grew up amidst ancient furniture, books in Latin, and human mummies, but none of those things made me melancholy, because I came into the world with a breath of the jungle in my memory. My father, an Indian with yellow eyes, came from the place where the hundred rivers meet; he smelled of lush growing things and he never looked directly at the sky, because he had grown up beneath a canopy of trees, and light seemed indecent to him. Consuelo, my mother, spent her childhood in an enchanted region where for centuries adventurers have searched for the city of pure gold the conquistadors saw when they peered into the abyss of their own ambitions. She was marked forever by that landscape, and in some way she managed to pass that sign on to me (1).

When students begin to inscribe their own identities through writing about landscapes of childhood, much spirit comes into their descriptive prose. For example:

> Our summer-filled days always began the same. After breakfast we rode our bikes around the driveway for a while, or maybe tossed the half-ripped baseball through the air, anxiously awaiting the thrill of seeing one more tuft of soggy grey stuffing escape and float like a feather to the ground. Mom sat on the back steps, keeping a cautious eye on all five of us, one hand nervously peeling the worn grey paint from her perch, the other soothingly caressing the neighbor's cat. We played all day with grass-stained skin and shoes so full of sand we could hardly walk (O'Malley 1).

Environmental autobiographies are not always idyllic. In a recent class of 15 students, two wrote about places in which they were molested as children. Whatever the effects of early landscape and environment on the adult character, beginning with such explorations can give students a base, a grounding, for other kinds of environmental writing. Knowing where we came from, how we grew into our present identities, gives us an honest sense of position and perspective on environmental issues — and helps liberate us from the illusion of the inviolate self floating through life.

In the Environmental Autobiography assignment I stress the individual identities of the students. This is a place where anger, sometimes even rage, can be appropriately expressed, especially in revealing deep personal memories of the physical landscapes of poverty. Here scenes of Indian reservations with a family surviving on prairie dogs, and of Black Southern neighborhoods without sewerage or electric power, find voice. But it is also true that we, despite separate backgrounds, are joined together in a social enterprise, a hope and a search for common ground. I do not leave a fuzzy, sentimental 'closure' over the class as a kind of official denial of the individuals' inscribed suffering. Rather, in the subsequent assignments, discussed below, we move together toward concrete solutions for environmental problems in specific cases. I assume and project an ideal of harmony and cooperation in specific landscapes, both cultural and physical. I do not presume to settle or decide the long-range movement of "our multicultural society," whatever that construct may turn out to be for each student in her personal future. But I know how to encourage the making of good stories from the painful, often silent, lives my students have led. And I know how to bring people together in problem-solving for very particular landscapes. Our discussions sometimes touch these questions of resistance v harmony, but we do not attempt totalizing solutions. I make no secret of my enthusiasm for our class, and I hope it may be a model for projects involving each writer — in strong personal voice — working with other people of diverse backgrounds, focused on particular intersections of community and terrain.

The Landscape History

Here the assignment is to take a particular site such as a house, farm, waterfront, or neighborhood woods, and follow it through time. Or one may take a group of people through time, and show how their treatment of the land changed. The inspirational model here is John Brinkerhoff Jackson, founder of the Landscape Studies field at Harvard. An excellent introduction is Janet Mendlesohn's documentary video on his life and work, "Figure in a Landscape" (Mendlesohn). One of Jackson's essays, "The Westward Moving House," traces several generations of a family through their houses.

Jackson begins in 16th century New England, moves through a generation on a midwest farm in the 19th century, and finally describes their contemporary descendants doing feedlot cattle farming in Texas. For each generation, Jackson focuses on the house and the ways it reflects and shapes the culture and psychology of the family. For example, of the Texans:

> Now is the slack time of the year, and every afternoon the two men and Ray's boy Don, and once in a while a neighbor, go to work on Ray's new house. It is being built out of the best grade cement block, brought by truck some two hundred miles, and it is to be absolutely the last word in convenience and modern construction. It is to be flat roofed and one story high, with no artistic pretensions, but intelligently designed. It is located on a barren and treeless height of land on the outskirts of town (Jackson 1970, 31).

Jackson points out that the home is temporary; like their farm, they think of their house as a transformer of energy, a node of secular convenience. They are as far from their God-fearing ancestors in the dark, bedeviled New England forest as they can be.

For her Landscape History project, one of my students studied the history of the beaches in her community on the Massachusetts coast. She incorporated library research and family interviews:

> A legend concerning the sand bar gives Horseneck Beach its name. The tale is of a man who lost track of time and stayed on the island past low tide. In an effort to get back to the mainland, he led his team of two oxen, a cart, and a lead horse across the bar when the tide was too high. Half-way across, the

cart began to float and the horse was lifted off its feet. The horse swam out into deep water, dragging the cart and the man along with it. The cart sank, and the horse and the man drowned. The oxen managed to break free from the cart and washed up into shallow water on Horseneck. They were half-drowned with the wooden yoke wrong side up on their necks. Men had to use ropes to pull them out from the undertow (Fazzina 2).

Another student researched the textile mills in Lowell, Massachusetts:

Beginning at the 6:00 am bell, the mill bustled with activity, each successive level in the factory serving a distinct phase of the manufacturing process. The "mill girls" labored on foot for eleven to fourteen hours per day, six days per week (Signorello 4).

Often students present their landscape history essays to the class along with old and new photographs. The relatively impersonal perspective of the historical study, following close upon the environmental autobiography, provides a balance and a sense of the possible interpretations of any landscape.

The Nature Essay

This form includes Thoreau's *Walden*, Annie Dillard's *Pilgrim at Tinker Creek*, and many of Barry Lopez's fine essays. The typical structure is that of a journey, in which the writer leaves civilization and travels into nature, has an encounter of some kind — with a wolf, a storm, an eclipse, etc. — and then returns bearing a new understanding. The time encompassed may be a few hours or an entire year, but the experience is usually reported as a seamless, intense encounter. In his essay, "The Stone Horse," Lopez recounts his solitary search in the California desert for a huge horse carved in stone by early native peoples:

> In the first moment of recognition I was without feeling. I recalled later being startled, and that I held my breath. It was laid out on the ground with its head to the east, three times life size. As I took in its outline I felt a growing concentration of all my senses, as though my attentiveness to the pale rose color of the morning sky and other peripheral images had now ceased to be important. I was aware that I was straining for sound in the windless air and I felt the uneven pressure of the earth hard against my feet. The horse, outlined in a standing profile on the dark ground, was as vivid before me as a bed of tulips (6-7).

One student wrote of her month-long experience as a governess to a seven-year-old Saudi prince, locked inside an exotic garden near Boston. She arrived and was ushered into an expanse of manicured roses:

> ...The flowers alone were incredible— big and bold, yet soft and serene, to allow the observer to take a closer look at their beauty. From afar the roses looked as if they were actually planted on the lustrous green plot of land. However, upon closer inspection one could clearly see the neat patch of soil needed for each to flourish. The colors reminded me of Easter and other pastel-celebrated occasions. Satiny shades of lilac, peach, champagne,

and cameo-pink surrounded a single row of pearl-white roses. Placed several feet away, there was a big white wicker chair with ample armrests and a nearby foot stand. I was tempted to sit down, but when I checked to see if anyone was watching, sure enough a man was coming toward me with a multitude of horticulture tools and accessories to make sure nothing was damaged.

He had a stern look on his face and wore a blue turban on his head. I thought for sure he was going to yell at me for standing so close. Instead, he delicately reached out and carefully plucked a single white rose from the center of the arrangement. I accepted the gift graciously and held the flower gently with both hands. While I took the stem with my left hand, my right hand caressed the velvetiness and delicacy of the soft petals. I looked up to thank him and he was already on the other side of the garden (Carroll 2).

For Barry Lopez in the essay cited above, the stone horse represents the desert landscape and its biological and cultural heritage. The monument's vulnerability to vandalism and careless tourism brings both writer and reader to reconsider our own actions and attitudes toward the earth. For Tracy Carroll, the rose garden comes to represent the elegant but tightly controlled web of social relations in Saudi life. She experiences the role of a woman under male eyes for a month — and finds her treatment highly ritualized and frustrating for an American used to expressing herself freely.

The Landscape Perception Study
This assignment involves formulating a research question and

investigating it through interviews. Many fine examples of such studies may be found in *Humanscape*, edited by Stephen and Rachel Kaplan. An extended account of the methods of research and evaluation that are possible is contained in the Kaplans' *The Experience of Nature*. Lawrence Holt and Diane Garvey's video documentary, "The Wilderness Idea," works well to introduce the diverse viewpoints that may compete for control of a single landscape.

This kind of project lends itself to teamwork. Four of my students combined their efforts to study the history of our university campus, focusing on the present-day feelings of the people whose land was taken by eminent domain when the institution was built in the 1960s. This passage is from their conclusion:

> Many years have passed since they lost their land and they have adjusted, but they still have feelings concerning the issue. It is very difficult and oftentimes painful to re-examine the past, but [these five people] have been extremely helpful and cooperative for the sake of this project.
>
> If there is one thing that we have discovered from our research, it is that this investigation is not truly complete until every previous owner has told his/her story (Carlson 10).

Environmental Writing in the Master's Thesis

Minority students have all experienced deep rifts between the physical and cultural landscapes they know, and those sung in the ideology of democratic America. Encouraged to explore this difference in their writing, they frequently rise to the task. Each kind of environmental writing discussed above may be used effectively. Examples from three projects follow.

James Edward Miller was a graduate student of great charisma. I worked with him in developing an Environmental Autobiography, and this process helped release a beautiful style which he later used in his master's thesis, an exposé of corrupt black and white politics in the building of a nuclear power plant in his rural Mississippi county. James had terrible problems with grammar and spelling. But because his writing was integral to both his growing, powerful new sense of self, and to the telling of his local environmental story, his confidence in the language bloomed. He wrote:

> An economy is a sometimes simple, sometimes complex set of institutions and social relationships that work to meet the material, social and cultural needs of its members. But it is also a system of power. Power is involved in decisions over who will get what, who will work for whom, and under what conditions (Miller 12).

Not only did James Miller write a clear, scathing indictment of corruption in Mississippi, he did it without compromising his energetic and fluid prose. In his thesis acknowledgments he said:

> [To] the proud people of Claiborne County, especially those who fought to bring about social change within a southern racist climate, at a time when such a social expression could have meant death.
> My deepest acknowledgment goes to Carolyn Turnipseed Miller, my friend, comrade and wife. I have benefited enormously from discussions with and encouragement from this sister. Her wisdom and understanding have put my social commitment into it's

proper perception. She has been like a ray of sunshine on the sometimes dark and bloody battlefield of community organizing.

May the Most High cherish and sustain this sister and may the winds of time always be at her back....my strength, my wife, my African Queen (1).

James Bluestone is a member of the Hidatsa Tribe. He is a person of intelligence, charm, and dignity, and all of these qualities show through in his writing. His master's thesis is a clear, passionate account of his tribal history and prospects:

1. INTRODUCTION: THE PROBLEMS

This paper is concerned with the economic recovery of the Three Affiliated Tribes from the impact of the Federal government flooding the Fort Berthold Indian Reservation in 1954. Today — thirty-two years later — the reservation has never recovered from their removal, their loss of prime lands, and their break-up of unity, communication and organization.

A. The State of Things Prior to the Dam

The bottomlands of the Fort Berthold Reservation, according to the reports of the Bureau of Indian Affairs done at the time of the taking act, abounded in natural resources. The naturally fertile alluvial soils, the natural shelter for the tribes' livestock herds, the abundant deposits of coal, the standing timber, the availability of seasonal fruits such as june berries and chokecherries, the extensive habitat for wild game as well as a plentiful supply of good water for domestic and stock watering purposes, all combined to provide a solid economic base that sustained the tribes, virtually independent

[of] the non-Indian economy around them. The tribal people for the most part, according to the Missouri River Basin Investigations (MRBI) reports, through a tradition of self-reliance and hard work, produced an income from their allotments, and from the common tribal lands, that made them economically self-sufficient (7).

Like Miller, Bluestone moved from personal writing to objective subjects without the deadening loss of self that accompanies so much scientific and technical prose. He found a way within his writing, to integrate his position in a unique place and time with his emerging professional life.

Linda D. Walton grew up in a small town in Missouri. When the white superintendent of her district finally accepted integration, he built a bonfire of the black high school's history — the pictures, the yearbooks, everything of valued memory went up in flames. This experience left Linda with a fierce determination to fight for educational equality. In her thesis writing she sought to reveal the basic needs of students as these are constitutionally guaranteed, then to plan for implementation:

The issue is not "better" compensatory education, or even "better" test scores; the issue is better education in the hour-to-hour and day-to-day interactions between students and the teachers who serve them.

The quest is for education that will challenge, inspire, and stretch students, while opening doors to new opportunities rather than screening them out with curriculum and tracking policies that constrain real learning growth (Walton 4).

My evolving courses in Nature, Landscape, and Environmental Writing have provided some of the most satisfying experiences of my teaching career. The disjunction between American dreams and realities drives the subject, and it is a joy to watch thoughtful students find endless ways of revealing themselves within the landscape, and the landscape within themselves.

Seven

Imagining a Balance of Nature

In the examples of conservation writing discussed so far, I chose the places described for personal reasons or they were assigned. The question of how to choose an appropriate site for conservation effort hasn't emerged as a problem. And while natural features and cultural traditions have been presented as reasons to value a place, the means of weighing these reasons hasn't been discussed. The first step could be expressed in the question:

What balance of nature exists currently in a site one is considering?

And the second as:

What balance does one wish there for the future?

The first question is empirical, to be answered by the best science available. The second is personal and cultural, and requires a story. Developing as a conservation writer isn't learning to check off a list of natural and cultural values; rather it's learning to feel one's way into a well researched and deeply experienced landscape. It's finding the right new metaphors and balances within one's emotional as well as rational judgments.

Once these questions have been resolved, a conservation writer may contribute to the political process which will settle the fate of the land.

Some Unhelpful Myths

Let's look at the way we make decisions about a balance of nature.

Ecologist Daniel B. Botkin, in his book *Discordant Harmonies*, draws upon experiences from a professional lifetime to show how false theories of the balance of nature have sometimes produced disastrous policies.

By pointing to ice sheets, volcanoes, and other disruptions of living systems, he argues there is no single mature state of an ecosystem one can call "natural." Among his most disturbing themes is arbitrary use of the terms "ecological succession" and "climax forest."

Botkin presents two myths of Western culture. Each derives from an ancient lineage and claims many supporters today, yet each is false. The first often serves as the broadest assumption of many developers; it is the belief that there is a balance of nature which humans cannot seriously undo, no matter what mischief we cause. The second, often an article of faith for conservationists, is that there is a balance of nature which humans can fatally disturb — and perhaps already have. Both parties believe in *some* concept of balance in nature. However, ecologists have recently come to recognize the pervasiveness of change, which presents problems for both myths.

Botkin discusses Tsavo, a 5,000 square mile national park in Kenya. When it became a park in 1948 its landscape was dry and flat, heavily forested but devoid of many large animals which had been killed around the turn of the century. David Sheldrick, its first warden, devoted years to building up the population of elephants and other species. He built thousands of miles of roads for tourist access, brought in water, and carried out an aggressive campaign against poachers. By 1959 he'd achieved too much success: the elephants were knocking down trees and turning the park into a lunar landscape.

Scientists were called in to study the situation. They recommended that 3,000 elephants be shot to keep the population within its food supply. Sheldrick nearly agreed, then reversed himself and fell back on his faith in the old balance of nature idea, including a natural ecological climax.

The park's trustees sided with Sheldrick, and the result was that the elephant population increased until it reached and surpassed the points which ecologists characterize as crisis, overshoot, crash, and die-off. The once-green park lay nearly lifeless. This result showed decisively that, at 5,000 acre scale in that place and time, change, not stability, was intrinsic to the ecological community. In hindsight we can say "yes, but humans put the fence around the park, and the elephants reproduced to the point of their own starvation. So this was a human-caused crisis." Sheldrick was trying to understand the elephant situation in terms of natural, not human, forces. The human hand was hidden, for the moment.

This example shows the fallacy in trusting that nature's balance will take care of itself. And yet a conservationist cannot help but fear that if change is admitted as intrinsic to nature, as "natural," then one can't argue against the changes developers want to make. All species come into existence and at some time disappear again. Furthermore, humans are animals and thus perfectly natural; so why shouldn't they eliminate a butterfly species to build a golf course (a California case), or destroy a small perch to widen a river (a Mississippi case)?

In response to such aggressive demands for the expansion of human territory, environmentalists frequently seize relative terms like "wilderness," "wild," "natural," and "balance," and treat them as absolutes. Writers may avoid facing intrinsic change by asserting a stubborn fundamentalism about the proper balance for a place.

Sometimes writers have relied on metaphors which embody balance-of-nature stories. These have included nature is divine order, nature is an organic creature, and nature is a great machine. Botkin includes helpful discussions of these myths in his book, and he argues that they reflect cultural perspectives, not objective truths.

Perhaps the most important lesson from Tsavo is that before we can talk about a balance of nature, we must consider the question: At what scale? The myth that nature will always correct its imbalances, like the myth that these cannot be corrected, can only be sustained by focusing on a landscape at a particular scale, while ignoring others. Tsavo was a reserve too small to support its population of elephants. The fence plus the hunting ban caused the problem, and the landscape could not restore itself.

Botkin says we must recognize our responsibility to choose the ecosystems we want — and not simply tell ourselves God or Nature has already created those which are good. Too much reliance on the idea of a 'climax' state of nature can make it seem natural, or even the goal of nature. Within evolutionary theory, however, nature has no goals. Individual organisms, and perhaps genes, strive to survive and reproduce. Natural selection, which is not a conscious process, determines the winners. Humans must shape ecosystems; we must choose and manage the balances of nature we want. In order to make rational choices about this we need science, and analysis of why we value certain features of ecosystems above others. This analysis isn't just a matter of listing natural values; it's also a matter of considering the stories we tell about places.

Balance and Rates of Change

Aldo Leopold, in his 1948 *A Sand County Almanac*, called for a land ethic, which would value a state of harmony between people and land. Botkin declares that he agrees with this, but wants to update the kind of knowledge needed to achieve harmony, and to clarify the concept of a *new* harmony. Whereas Leopold had repeated the ideas of forest succession and climax forest as natural goods, Botkin shows how forests and other ecosystems change in response to unpredictable events. These can be natural, like hurricanes and fires, or cultural, like fences and hunting activities. To claim goodness for a particular pattern of ecosystem stability, then, requires more than uncritical reliance on an earlier balance of nature concept.

One key idea in the new harmony is that we should manage not for *no* change to the climax states we value, but for *slow* change. We should be conservatives: we ought to honor complex states of nature, and our own future needs, by protecting the life we find. It shouldn't be necessary to declare a climax state sacred, in order to argue against its destruction. One biologist with whom I discussed Botkin's ideas said he still thinks the notions of succession and climax are useful heuristic concepts; that is, they often serve to accurately organize our observations of an ecosystem over time, but he agrees we shouldn't treat climax states as holy, and we should find other arguments to protect them. In the essay on John Muir I show how a century ago he used religious language to characterize nature and create an audience for conservation work. This can be effective as metaphor, but rather than attempt to freeze the metaphor into literal doctrine, today's writer needs to describe the non-doctrinal spiritual response people often have to climax states of nature. Spirituality is related to our perceptions of beauty, and to our psychological need for quiet landscapes. There is no shame in admitting cultural and personal elements within the use of relative terms like "spiritual," "sacred," "holy," "the wild," "wilderness," and "beautiful landscapes." To say these terms are relative is to say they take their meaning from their contexts, including the brain of the observer, as well as from nature observed.

Writing at Three Scales

Conservation Writers usually work at one of three scales: global, regional or local. Problems like global warming, acid rain, and songbird declines are global in scale, and must be addressed through consciousness raising and political action. Consciousness raising may be done through journalism; political action may be achieved through op/ed advocacy for specific initiatives. In my woodcock essay, I tried to link a local New England coastal landscape to migration patters of a bird which travels from Canada to Mexico. My piece was aimed at consciousness raising, and though it recommended protection of wet woods, it wasn't part of a specific policy initiative to reverse decline.

At regional scale, such as a large watershed, one might work on threats to a species across all or most of its habitat. In "River of Silence," I report working on a river which flowed through six towns. A project that size requires state level help, and coordination among towns.

In representing the interests of citizens at this scale, a writer should seek information about the position of each species in a tree of kinship to other species. The writer should consider all species present, and approximate populations of each. This is a point of law. Both federal and state governments have endangered species laws. These respect uncommonness and precariousness. So if one is working at this scale, and representing public interests, one must seek the available knowledge about how each organism fits with all others, and how the region as habitat fits with others. For example, are any resident species endemic, which is to say, found only here? One can use scientific techniques to study the infrequency of a species, and the shortage of its habitat.

By locating a species precisely within a great historical narrative about all life, systems biologists create a library of the living world as well as its past. This library not only allow rational decisions about what species and habitats are most rare, and thus most in need of protection, it also shows us the detailed history of our own appearance and changes on earth.

The third scale of conservation writing, that of particular places that can be walked and watched and heard and tasted, calls for a writer's more independent perceptions. A writer may work as a volunteer for a land trust, a conservation commission, a community planning initiative, or for local chapters of The Sierra Club, The Audubon Society, or another non-profit. One may also work as a reporter for a newspaper or magazine, and approach local nature as part of a beat. A writer may gather information from people with local knowledge in order to protect community landscapes, species and water quality. Such research and visits to the land can contribute to personal, intimate representation of a valued place.

From Pets to Wild Animals to Life on Earth

Most people with a passion for land conservation come to that interest through a childhood love of the animals, birds, fish, insects, plants, and trees near their homes. They may first awaken to the needs of wild animals through the love of a dog or cat. Through sensing the feelings of a pet we may come to wish all nature were respected, and we may feel especially that animals with complex nervous systems must experience pleasure and pain just as we do. This, we may feel, gives them value and certain rights, such as the right not to be cruelly treated. Thus we may care about a particular environmental cause, like the annual slaughter of young seals in Nova Scotia, based on our feelings for the creatures as individuals; photographs of the so-called harvest of baby seals may well remind us of childhood pets.

This childhood interest often grows into adult conservation work, and leads some people to become ecologists. These biologists do fieldwork at local or community scale, observing individual creatures and testing hypotheses about their relationships. Such scientists seek to discover energy flows between members of just a few species; these observers work with individual organisms, keenly aware of the difference between, say, a particular whitetail deer with a recognizable face, and the species called "whitetail deer." While systems biologists focus on the genetic information coded into each living organism, and seek to place this information in a historical narrative about life on earth, ecologists focus on the organism's behavior, its population dynamics, and its community interactions. In what ways does it compete with other organisms, and in what ways does it cooperate?

Both sorts of specialists know that their studies intersect in the living organism, which is a vessel of information inherited from distant time, yet which is alive in space along with myriad other organisms which it will support or resist from moment to moment.

A conservation writer may come to the task of land protection from a background like that of the ecologist, and find the living beings of the natural world interesting and varied and beautiful. DNA and systems of relationship with other species may seem of secondary importance, at least from an emotional point of view. After all, why conserve anything unless it's alive and can move and interact and have feelings?

There are people whose conservation goal is the protection of all living beings. Some groups embrace an ethical stance based upon Deep Ecology, including the principle that all life has equal value.

If a writer held such a viewpoint and wanted to choose a place to spend effort advocating for protection, the criterion might be simply: How many animals live here? Or, perhaps: How many animals and plants live here? It might not seem necessary to consider genera, species, or sets of genes, or make efforts to protect biological diversity. Differences between organisms don't matter to some people — only the creatures' abilities to feel pleasure and pain, or with plants, their abilities to grow and reproduce.

But most people wish to protect biological diversity, not just living animals and plants but also the genetic heritage of life on earth. That means protecting the DNA of species that are rare, including the DNA of some that are unappealing. Who wants to devote resources to conserving viruses, bacteria, beetles, spiders, scorpions and snakes? Most people want to make sure we protect the large and appealing species, the so-called 'charismatic megafauna,' like bears, lions, and eagles. Before preferences can even be discussed, we must have a rich inventory of the life in a potential reserve.

Writers in their Habitats

Writers seem solitary experts when we read their works, such as the essays of John Muir or Rachel Carson. As readers we imagine they know the facts about the places they describe, possess a clear point of view as to the value of those places, and take us with their narrative skill into the heart of nature. With such images of writers in mind, we might well feel intimidated. How could we ever come to such knowledge? A red-tailed hawk hunts in my field. It shines magnificently in the sunshine, floating on the breeze, studying the grass for a mouse or a small bird. I think of it as a single being, lord of its space. But of course it only exists as part of a reproducing population; it carries a DNA history older than the dinosaurs; and my snapshot views of it don't unravel its ecological relationships.

Just as the hawk represents its history and community, flying and hunting for its brief, glorious moment in time, a writer comes to nature within a certain social and cultural network. Fortunately we don't need to do our own science, which would usually be impossible. But we do need to understand how to research the work of others, and how to place the reasons people give for protecting a particular balance of nature into historical and ethical contexts. The social groups that produce us, and that we reproduce, are part of our habitats.

I gather information in a variety of ways. Sometimes it's by knowledge developed in childhood; sometimes by using the web; sometimes by listening to experts; and sometimes by researching and conversing with people from a different culture.

But suppose a writer wants to approach the task of conservation more systematically. What if one has several opportunities for conservation writing, but limited time, and must choose between them?

Ideally, the writer will have access to a species inventory. This means teams of observers go into the field on a given day, and note every species observed, and the number of creatures belonging to each. The Audubon Society sends out volunteers once a year for the Christmas Count of birds. Its website reports the results, and can help people in making decisions. For example, knowledge of just how important one's small patch of land might be as habitat for a species (like woodcocks) could determine whether to protect it or build another house on it. Knowing woodcocks are disappearing at the rate of 2% per year also might lead a hunter to retire his shotgun.

A large species inventory project is in the works for the Great Smokey Mountains National Park. Over 10-15 years, many groups will cooperate to survey half a million acres and an estimated 100,000 species.

These two inventory projects assay land at large scales. Often a writer will be concerned with a much smaller area. Discovering the number of species in a single site yields a measure of richness that ecologists call Alpha Diversity. For example, suppose I walked a path, or transect, in the 3 acres of wet woods behind my house, and noted the species at regular intervals. Imagine that I saw 7 bird species, 5 mammal species, 20 insect species, and 25 species of plants and trees. This would yield an Alpha Diversity number of

57.

Three miles from here my town owns 26 acres of conservation land. Suppose I walked a transect there and found 50 of the same species, and 5 different ones. Adding the five species found only in the town woods to the seven found only in mine, yields a Beta Diversity number of 12.

Finally, if we take all the separate habitat areas within a wide geographic region, and add the total number of species found in them, we obtain a number representing Gamma Diversity. Continuing the example above, that number is 62 — the 57 species in the first patch, plus the five new ones in the second patch.

Once we have an idea of the species richness of a patch (Alpha), of the relative richness of several patches in the area (Beta), and of all the patches in a wide geographic region (Gamma), we can begin to form one idea of the region's ecological significance.

These measures are based on observations of living organisms. But an inventory of species relationships can be obtained by looking at parts of animals and plants, through genetic testing. One version, the work of over 500 scientists around the world, is available at the Tree of Life web project (http://tolweb.org/tree/phylogeny.html).

Making One's Own Rules

Suppose you own a single acre which is Alpha rich, and which you love. This was the situation of writer Joy Williams on Siesta Key, Florida. When she needed to sell her property, many people tried to convince her to simply take the highest bid, walk away, and let the new owners bulldoze everything and put up the five houses which the zoning allowed. But she put a conservation easement on the property, restricting uses and protecting the vegetation, and held on until she found the right buyers. She took much less money for her land, but was glad to do so. She writes about this beautifully in "One Acre: On Devaluing Real Estate to

Keep Land Priceless," in the anthology *Listening to Earth*, ed. by Hallowell and Levy.

Williams admits that her valuation of the wild creatures on her property was deeply personal and emotional. Her invitational descriptions sing with the power of names, as in "There was bougainvillea, azalea, gardenia, power puff and firecracker plant, crotons, wild lilies, sea grape, and several orchid trees."

Her acre was Alpha rich, though probably other patches in the region sheltered the same species; so perhaps it was Beta poor. She didn't care. She knew she could sell the land at the highest price, sacrifice the inhabitants to development, and donate the money to a conservation group like The Nature Conservancy; she knew they could spend it buying land within a larger block, which they might believe would better protect inhabitants. That strategy might save more organisms, and species, in the long run. But it might not. Should she trust her own knowledge of this special place, or turn the decision over to others, who were factoring many properties in a complex calculation?

Conservation requires love of specific places and creatures, not just quantitative analysis. Williams concludes, "I wanted more than money for my land, more than the mere memory of it, the luxury of conserving it sentimentally and falsely through lyrical recall. I wanted it to be."

Williams loved her acre, and as a private landowner she controlled its fate.

Elements of Good Judgment

Emotions are a part of conservation decisions, though reason and science are as well. Every conservation project, every written appeal, involves both an objective claim about what lives there and a subjective claim about why the reader should care. So before a writer begins, before the first word goes down, there must be research (maybe walking transects, maybe visiting a website like Audubon's, sometimes just talking to people more familiar with the area), and there must be judgment. This judgment will reflect cultural and personal elements, but also scientific ones. In the end, after research and consultation with others, a writer must choose whether the place in question is in reasonable shape now, and is likely to remain so, or whether it is threatened with a particular imbalance and requires action.

Cultural values, such as our preference for historical periods — for example the way forests looked to early European explorers — or our desire to protect a single endangered species at the expense of others — must be admitted into the debate. We prefer certain species to others. Bears, lions, and eagles are more popular than roaches, scorpions, and snakes. Baby animals, with their rounder faces, are more popular than adults. Some plants, like orchids, seem treasures; others, like dandelions, seem weeds.

We must integrate scientific inventories of sites, clear reasons to value places, and a keen sense of our audiences' desires. We should take responsibility for our conceptualizations of nature through understanding the histories of our myths and metaphor systems, and the stories we wish to tell about ourselves within landscapes. These stories will blend natural and cultural elements, but they are not subjective or equal. Attention to detail, reportage of history and current status, and care in the writing to avoid clichés at the concept level, lead not only to superior writing, but to superior ecological planning.

Eight

Conservation's Observer Problem

The Observer in Ecology

Beyond the light of my desk lamp and computer screen, and the hum of my air conditioner, there exists a coastal hardwood swamp of great mystery. Though I live in the old settled East, not far from Providence and Boston, even closer to Fall River and New Bedford, my garden and lawn connect to a greenbelt teeming with wild life. Coyotes cry to the stars at night, hunt the deer in corridors of wet green, and raid sheep farms in town. Foxes visit my deck when it's late and quiet, delicately feasting on sunflower seeds I've spilled for the birds. In daylight, red-tailed hawks float above the treetops, searching for rabbits and songbirds in the dense growth below. Sometimes eagles drift up there as well.

The life surrounding us appears as a matrix of information, presenting some events which fit our expectations, and others which do not. In order to focus on one set of relationships, we must exclude others. An ecological study of coyotes in my county must leave out earthworms; as a biologist friend wades the coastal waters collecting invading crabs, and examines their stomach contents to explore impacts on prey species, she ignores ospreys circling above, and mosquitoes grazing her ear. Choices call before the first hypothesis can be tested.

What then gets chosen? How are some species selected and highlighted? Why are others consigned to the background of scientific attention? These are aspects of ecology's observer problem. We are used to such a concept in physics, where we understand that spatial and temporal measurements are relative to an observer's position. And we may realize that in anthropology, the attitude of an ethnographer shapes interviewee responses. But we're so accustomed to viewing familiar scenes of park or garden, or the turns of a local trail, as nature that exists with or without us, that we're tempted to imagine all nature in such static pictures. What has this tableau to do with us? Wouldn't it be the same whether we observe it or not? And shouldn't it be possible to inventory all species present in such an elegant, well-ordered scene?

In their book, *Toward a Unified Ecology*, Timothy F.H. Allen and Thomas W. Hoekstra discuss what we might call an open secret at the heart of ecology. This is that a human observer determines what is recognized and studied, and in this sense valued. The same person who includes certain animals and plants within a frame of reference necessarily excludes other species from the framework.

In Physics, we recognize that measurements of the position and speed of subatomic particles are relative to the observer's position. By contrast, Allen and Hoekstra write, "The things we study in ecology seem very real. Nevertheless, ecology is a science and is therefore about observation and measurement more than about nature independent of observation" (13).

This applies to the things studied, and to those left out.

> Even at the grossest level of decision making, when the ecologist chooses what to study, that act influences the outcome

of the investigation. When one chooses to
study shrews, there is an implicit decision
not to study everything else. In that implicit
decision most other things ecological, such
as trees, rivers, or ants, are excluded from the
data (13).

Allen and Hoekstra remind us of the story that the
entire army of Alexander the Great slept beneath a single
Banyan tree. Is this true? It depends upon the observer's
viewpoint: the Banyan extends thin rootlets which touch the
ground and begin to thicken and spread roots. Eventually they
appear as new trunks. Genetically identical to the original
tree, they become either its spatial extensions or an entirely
new forest, depending upon one's perspective. Perhaps for
a biologist they would be a single tree, while for the army
being sheltered beneath the many trunks and branches, they
would be a forest.

These examples show that the concept of the
observer's position includes more than spatiotemporal
location. It encompasses interests, needs, and a way of
focusing attention. This way implies a cultural matrix, a
language, and a community of investigators.

Every project proposed by developers rests upon
a framework which includes implicit claims about which
species matter. To the timber corporations of the American
northwest, Pine, fir, and cedar are interesting, while spotted
owls are a nuisance. All our activities take place within frames
of ecological reference; by attending to how ecologists,
developers, planners and others specify these, we may learn to
see our role as decision-makers about the ecosystems around
us. After all, while local nature is 'out there' in an objective
sense, frames of ecological reference are the stage sets upon
which environmental debates are dramatically enacted. Scale
within the framework is determined by grain and extent of
the data. Grain determines how small the observed data will

be, while extent determines their largest possible size in time and space. Scale in this sense is not about 'the world out there,' but is about our measuring conventions. Scientific stories are limited in this way, as are all stories.

Allen and Hoekstra point out that definitions are primary. Before we can discuss change, we must identify static frames of reference within which change occurs. (For example, if we study change for one year on a farm, we must first draw a line at the edge of the farm property, and another at the end of the year, and pretend not to notice what happens outside this zone.) But as the example about shrews, ants, trees, and rivers shows, specifying an ecological frame of reference always leaves much out, and hence is relative to personal/cultural observer positions. These choices of what to focus upon are subjective in the sense that other options exist initially, but once the choices are made the observations which follow are objective.

The Observer Problem in Conservation

Which species claim our attention determines what we see at a given place and time. The knowledge we eventually generate helps determine how others act there, and what environmental policies are adopted. A study of bears might bring hunters; a discovery of rare plants might halt development. If we ignore a species, its uniqueness may be lost in the ethos of change and transformation that grips our time.

Cultural and political interests are involved. Scientists often specialize in organisms which the wider society has blessed with funding: mountain lion, condor, elegant osprey. In these cases beauty and scarcity lead a biologist to describe a place, on a certain day, as the habitat of this creature alone. Selection of a few organisms from a rich matrix is necessary before ecological study can begin.

A parallelism holds in the field of conservation. Whether one looks at planet Earth from a satellite 40 miles high and sees exploding cities eating green space alive, or takes a drive around one's own town and counts the white ends of plastic pipe (percolation tests for new house sites) it is evident that development continues rapidly. Conservationists can save less territory now because land prices have risen so dramatically. It has become critical to pick one's battles. Out of the surrounding matrix of environmental problems, upon which shall I focus my energy and time?

Ecology and conservation arise within cultural and political situations. A complex weave of factors brings scientist or conservationist to subject and site. These factors will include society's long-term interests in educating people one way rather than another, and local, shorter-term urgencies concerning bulldozers, chain saws, and the disappearance of species. Ecologist and conservationist, by professional custom, respond to slowly deteriorating conditions in the informational matrix. (Without this general situation their roles would hardly have arisen at all.) Within this framework, each project they undertake will address limited windows of opportunity for knowledge or protection. In short, they respond to dynamic, unstable situations, in which effective storytelling holds a key to success.

Both ecologist and conservation writer frame particular species within a limited region of time and space for a study. But whereas a scientist contrasts known factors (constants) with unknown ones (variables) in an effort to discover whether a specific relationship exists, a conservationist seeks to preserve or restore a status quo. This does not mean a no-change zone, where evolution is halted, but rather a slow-change zone, where humans interfere minimally with species relations.

Just what choices must be made before a slow-change zone can be responsibly defined? At a fairly abstract level, a common prime directive for conservation work is 'protect diversity.' This principle alone does not tell us what to do in a specific situation, because there are different kinds of diversity, and because reasonable people can disagree about strategy and tactics. But in its very generality, the principle 'protect diversity' may allow stakeholders in an environmental discussion to proceed toward an agreed goal. This convergence is part of the urgency conservationists feel about the world today; it is also connected to the words 'conserve,' 'conservationist,' and 'conservative': all arise in relation to a valued state of affairs in which diversity is threatened.

Proceeding from this common point, we must ask in any given case whether the best path is 'hands off' an ecosystem, or whether we ought to take actions to encourage some species and discourage others. Even small, unobtrusive actions, like filling a bird feeder with seed, or opening the door to release a cat for the day, have dramatic effects when combined with the similar actions of millions of people.

One way of describing this situation is to say that almost every part of the natural world is a landscape for somebody. And landscapes are cultural and political entities as well as ecological ones. As J.B. Jackson has put it, "A landscape is...a space deliberately created to speed up or slow down the process of nature. As Eliade expresses it, it represents man taking upon himself the role of time" (Jackson 1984, 319.)

If we viewed Earth from the space shuttle we would be frightened by the spreading of cities. From an airplane over the American Midwest, one is amazed by vast fields of cropland — monocultures for food and profit. On foot, walking in parks or even wilderness areas, we respond emotionally to large trees with open vistas beneath — landscapes encouraged for their scale, which is to say our scale. Each approach to Earth reveals humans in control of nature, human time imposed upon, and altering the processes of, evolution.

When we think about what is happening to Earth as a whole, we recognize the need to plan conservation actions with several different time scales in mind. Events at different time scales differently effect habitats at different spatial scales. Ecologists distinguish three kinds of diversity: alpha, beta, and gamma. Alpha diversity means species diversity within a patch of land; beta diversity indicates diversity between several patches in the same area; gamma diversity indicates diversity on a regional scale, which includes many mosaics of land patches.

Clearly we need to know as much as possible about the gamma-diversity situation of species. Lacking this knowledge we might attempt to maximize diversity within a single patch, which might have reverse effects from the ones desired, because many species, such as deer, grouse, and crows, thrive on diversity within patches, and other species, such as the Florida scrub jay, can only thrive in relatively nondiverse plant communities, and then only in small numbers. So even though a patch of earth over which we have influence (like the woods and marsh behind my house) might be a tempting framework for a conservation plan, a wiser perspective would encompass my entire town and the watershed beyond.

Alpha, beta, and gamma diversity are concepts applicable to nature at many scales. Within these, choices must be made regarding grain and extent. Even then, once a region and its critical species are listed, the principle 'protect diversity' requires us to imagine different management strategies. In imagining policies for my wetland, differences appear depending whether I advocate for the deer or the coyotes, the rabbits or the foxes. From a logical point of view, an infinite number of perspectives on a single ecosystem are possible. This infinity of choices can seem bewildering, even debilitating. But only if one clings to a simple model of nature and culture, or hopes for a simple metaphor like those which guided our ancestors, such as nature is divine order, nature is an organic creature, and nature is a great machine.

Every choice within ecology and conservation, just

as those within development activities, requires creativity. Every action, and every restraint upon action, requires design decisions. This design ultimately includes physical treatment of land, but it begins with the writing process, where old metaphors are analyzed and new ones tried out.

Suppose I wish to make a narrow trail through the easternmost acre of my woods. Here the land is spongy and mossy, and the vegetation is dominated by shad blow, haw, holly, and shrub-sized bushes and trees growing in thickety profusion. A human can't walk through most of this, and a deer doesn't often choose to. If I cut a trail for my own exploring, and to draw the large mammals through, this will favor them but harm species which need shelter from them. Probably the deer, coyotes, foxes, raccoons, opossums, and neighborhood dogs have enough paths from which to invade tangles and swampy patches. In the past few years pheasant, quail and woodcock have become scarce, and I'm sure members of these species would appreciate (if they could) my not cutting such a path. I reach for a new metaphor like home is foxless, to guide my action. Here I combine the connotations of home, the warm modern sense of which only arose in 18th Century Holland (Rybcinski), with ecological knowledge about a specific place.

Consider a habitat which includes 'edge effects,' as most do. This is a concept promoted in 1933 by Aldo Leopold as beneficial to wildlife, and widely adopted as a management strategy. Leopold thought junctures of fields and forests, streams and uplands, even trails and thickets, provide advantages to many species. This is true, but not for all. By defining 'wildlife' as 'game species,' managers often rationalized breaking up uniform habitats into diverse patches; more deer and grouse were frequently the predictable and desired result, but lost in this 'edge effect' planning were many unnoticed, non-game species.

If one imagines a boundary between habitat types, it may be tempting to think of this line as a 'real' feature of nature, but as biologists William S. Alverson, et al., point out, such a line can only be defined by the experiences of particular organisms. Nearness to the line will produce a range of events of varying intensity.

Ecological field studies sometimes record the number of times particular organisms approach such a line. From these data points, an 'isoacme' map can be drawn to show average intensities at the same average densities from the line. Such displays are different for each species considered. Perhaps this is a useful way of illustrating how differently each species 'evaluates' edge effects in its habitat. This underscores the critical importance of being chosen as a key species for a study. It's unlikely that creatures omitted from study will have their interests considered in plans resulting from the study.

We noted that a study of foxes may leave out earthworms, and that Alexander's army slept beneath one or many Banyan Trees, depending on an observer's viewpoint. But how many species are really left out of particular studies, either in biology or planning?

Species numbers are greater than we are accustomed to thinking. In the 43 year period from 1940-1983, five new bird species were discovered every two years (Alverson, et al, 20). New species of mammals are now found at the rate of about five per year. Oceanic exploration for new life forms has just begun, bringing news of new whales and sharks, and deep-sea communities of sulfur- and methane-eating organisms. Biologist Terry Erwin and colleagues, working with associates in the 1970s studying rain forest trees, discovered each individual tree contained huge numbers of arthropod species, the spiders — and each tree contained unique species. Extrapolations from his data have led to estimates that the undiscovered arthropod species on Earth number from five to 30 million.

If we turn to smaller organisms the surprises are even greater. Studies of bacterial DNA in a single gram of beech-forest soil in Norway turned up between four and five thousand species. Examination of a gram of soil from the shallow seas off Norway's coast revealed an equal number, but virtually all of them were different from those in the forest sample.

These examples remind us that Earth's biological diversity is largely unknown, and that we miss whole realms of life by operating within many of our ordinary frames of reference. It's not only beetles and spiders that go extinct through massive rain forest burning — cases we hear about but may find emotionally distant. What about the newly discovered life forms around oceanic vents? Are these impacted by ocean dumping? What of the new bird species discovered every year? Are we destroying their habitats before we see them?

Birds are often omitted from our ecological planning considerations because of their migratory habits. We know that continued suburban development destroys habitats and encourages predatory species like blue jays, brown-headed cowbirds, and seagulls. Small, beautiful warblers are often the losers as 'edge effects' spread across the planet. Yet birds receive little consideration in many planning decisions, simply because they 'pass through' and their relation to a particular site may be difficult to establish.

All this indicates that every choice of an observer's position is fraught with consequences. And yet without such a choice there can be no observations, data-gathering, theorizing, or planning — for development or research or conservation. Once an ecological frame is chosen, and specified in both extent and grain, a discussion can begin about appropriate goals for this part of the natural world. And eventually diverse goals can find their way into a plan. But plans never spring from a void. They arise in response to threats and opportunities for conservation. Selecting a frame in space, including valued organisms within it, leads directly to concern with time — both the time of evolution past, which produced the place, and the cultural time which affects it now.

The next question is what target event the conservation writer has in mind. Sometimes this will be a vote (in a small community, a congress, a parliament, or another organization); at other times it will be an executive policy decision. Such pivotal moments determine whether ecosystems are protected or lost. Conservation work, like science, requires that a writer frame a region of space-time (extent), specify entities within that region (grain), and point to events projected into the future. For science, the effort is to observe these events; for the conservation writer, to influence them. (This is simplistic, of course: conservation biology as well as conservation writing require both descriptive and prescriptive components.)

The observer problem is a purely formal one: any story must begin with a specification of what is to be talked about, and with exclusions from the discussion. This means that conservation writers, like ecologists, must make choices before they can begin their work. Sometimes these involve ethical and aesthetic commitments, and always they involve practical and cultural commitments. The responsibility is great, because the entire task of conservation writing is to convince others to feel, think, and act toward a part of nature as you do.

'Solving' the observer problem is not a question of knowing everything about an ecosystem; that would be impossible because every viewpoint, every frame story, is limited. I have discussed the observer problem in ecology, conservation, and in storytelling. While there is no escape from the formal requirement that every narrative, or story, specify what it concerns, this does not pose an impossible problem for the conservation writer. In the following essay I examine the cultural values guiding many choices.

Nine

Choosing Landscape Values

In *A Sand County Almanac*, Aldo Leopold proposed that we extend ethical thinking and action from fellow human beings to nature. "An ethic, ecologically," he wrote, "is a limitation on freedom of action in the struggle for existence." Limiting our activities for the sake of other species, and their habitats, he called "a land ethic." When Leopold wrote these words they sounded strange, but half a century later many people embrace the idea. In our wetlands and woods, in our gardens and ponds, we take pleasure in restraint to protect nature.

The land ethic is widely embraced, as is the land aesthetic — guiding our efforts to promote landscape beauty. Yet these are only the starting points of land protection activities. How do we make practical decisions about when to leave a site completely alone, and when to introduce mowing or planting, for example? And what happens when the needs of different species conflict — how can we choose between them? A first step might be to list the cultural and natural values one respects. Later, one might revise the list as one's understanding grows.

Cultural Values

When management strategies like mowing, thinning, and stream-clearing are undertaken for aesthetic goals, one must choose the historical moment whose 'look' is sought. Consider two brief cases which illustrate this:

On Cape Cod, state park rangers needed a policy and management plan to protect a new acquisition for the park system. The landscape included fields, woods, and several historic houses. Planners chose the date of origin of a single one of these houses, then sought to make the surrounding landscapes conform to the way they had looked in that period. It wasn't possible to preserve the landscape aesthetics of all the houses; the attempt to do so would have resulted in a patchwork of views and ecological states lacking coherence. As Elizabeth R. Lehr showed in an article for my graduate class, by selecting a single period for guidance in landscape practices, the rangers achieved a measure of ecological and aesthetic unity. This example shows how historic preservation is subtly entwined with nature conservation.

Consider the Boundary Waters Canoe Area Wilderness in Minnesota. Some areas of this park are maintained so that a canoeist may glide along beneath huge trees with an open understory. To the uninitiated, this experience seems to touch 'true wilderness.' But actually management practices have created and sustained the forest in this 'climax stasis' condition; it mimics the ecosystem and aesthetics of the historical moment when European fur trappers first contacted the indigenous people of the region. The forest is magnificent, visually satisfying, and offers the visitor a sense of travel back in time to an unspoiled day. Although reserve designers made a good choice in their historic date for landscape practices, their cleverness in erasing subsequent history — power lines and cleared fields, for example — might tempt the visitor to imagine there was no previous history. In other words, the canoeist might believe these park-like forest banks embody a natural ideal which persists indefinitely. In the 18th Century and before, they were probably shaped by Native Americans through seasonal burning.

When one first embarks on a land conservation project it is tempting to imagine one is saving nature 'as it ought to be.' But usually this goal includes an aesthetic component — nature 'as it ought to look.' And the first question is: When? Any answer involves cultural history. This, in turn, requires choices: not every moment of past succession, or landscape configuration, can be represented.

An important part of the conservation task is historic preservation; to achieve this consistently, one must choose a date and manage for the 'correct look of that history.' Such choices shouldn't discourage us. They are part of the creative challenge of conservation, and they give us a meaningful role to play in the unfolding of nature. We can't avoid this role, but we can enjoy it.

Natural Values

Some conflicts cannot be evaded. For example, recently Massachusetts land managers had a painful choice between actions to support sea gulls or piping plovers. A 'no action' policy would support the gulls.

Similarly, in western Massachusetts, managers had to face the fact that domestic dogs were killing numbers of deer. 'No action' would have supported the dogs.

With regard to any piece of property one can choose:

      (1) to make the needs of a single species paramount (e.g., an endangered species);

      (2) to craft policies which will favor several species, ranked in a particular order;

      (3) one may attempt what is called 'integrated management,' in which one seeks a rough balance of (a limited number of) species needs, without selecting any one of these for special

treatment;

(4) we may treat a parcel as a baseline in a scientific study, which means it must be left alone, no matter what happens. While this sounds attractive and appeals to our 'pure wilderness' desire, in reality it means never compensating for natural events we dislike, such as devastating invasions of exotic species, windstorm damage, and fire.

Just as in the case of cultural values, the stewardship of natural values requires choices.

States of Nature versus Rates of Change

Early in this century ecologists came to believe in the idea of forest succession: that every forest goes through stages until it reaches a grand 'climax' state. This idea was applied to all sorts of ecosystems, with the result that each one was believed to have a proper, final, long-lasting, and most favorable stage. It became the goal of conservation to identify and protect such climax states of nature.

Recently ecologists have realized that much of the focus on preserving climax states was really driven by aesthetics, as in the case of the Boundary Waters Canoe Area discussed above. In the real world, climax states change eventually, perhaps in response to hurricanes, fires, earthquakes, volcanoes, diseases, or invasion by exotics; they often shift dynamics, restarting the clock and beginning a new succession, in response to influences like bulldozers and chainsaws.

What this means for conservationists is that we should protect slow rates of change, rather than no change at all. We need an historical account of each parcel including intelligent guesses about where it will trend with, and without, our interventions. Our goal should be wise stewardship of slow rates of change. Toward this understanding, some land trusts have begun to compile histories for the places they protect.

The Grand and the Pretty

In her 1997 book *Placing Nature*, landscape ecologist Joan Iverson Nausauer discusses the need for conservationists to appeal to aesthetic tastes and principles shared by their audiences. Americans are deeply committed to two distinct 'looks' for the natural world, which Nausauer calls 'grand' and 'pretty.' Grand landscapes feature broad rolling green fields framed in the distance by tall trees. They mimic 18th Century English estates, the sort designed by Humphery Repton and Capability Brown. Such landscapes, beyond the financial reach of most citizens, grace campuses, parks, golf courses, and grounds of the wealthy.

The other ideal, 'pretty,' lies within everyone's grasp. This is the look of a small but carefully tended lawn, garden, or window box. The pursuit of such landscapes often leads to faithful mowing, weed whacking, pruning and raking.

Two common features should be noted about these styles: first, they express care for nature, and signal that their owner is a careful person. We've all heard stories about people who 'let their place go' — refusing to mow, or make other concessions to community's look. Despite good intentions, say to provide habitat, in the end such people are regarded much like those who never cut their hair. They lose their place at the table of community conversation about how landscapes should be treated (see Pollan).

The other common feature of these two styles is that they can enhance, or destroy, environmental values. That is to say, neither style is good or evil, from a conservation perspective. To decide whether our gardens, lawns and woodlots, in conforming to these aesthetic ideals, are helping or hurting species, and encouraging a particular balance of nature, requires careful attention to each site.

When we appeal to our neighbors for a certain look for a conserved landscape, we will have deeply-rooted culture on our side if we cast our argument in terms of one of the dominant styles. If we can find a way to combine either,

107

or both, with such practices as leaving some areas entirely alone, audiences will feel more comfortable.

Conclusions

These are some of the kinds of information one needs to form clear and consistent conservation goals, strategies, and management plans. Not to discuss such matters leads to 'no action,' which of course is an action — one which supports current trends, whatever they are.

We might approach each parcel in two stages: the first to gather information of these kinds, and the second to discuss and choose goals, strategies, and plans. Ideally, we need information from many sources, such as neighbors of the property, oral histories of the town, stories from hunters and fishers, and so forth. We also need the perspectives of professional ecologists, biologists, landscape planners, and others.

Initially, each stage might be approached thus:

Stage One
1. Describe the place at landscape scale (that is, the way it appears to humans):
   A. Include natural features, such as landform, species, and tree of life information;
   B. Include cultural features, such as agriculture, stone walls and buildings.
2. Give the history of the place.
   A. Include human factors, such as farming uses;
   B. Include non-human factors, such as plant successions;
   C. Describe rates of change for species in the past.
3. Describe conflicts:
   A. Between species;
   B. Between other species and the human

species.
4. List possible land stewardship goals, such as:
   A. Management for a certain stage of nature (through annual mowing or flooding, for example);
   B. Management to encourage a particular succession;
   C. Management to encourage a particular rate of succession;
   D. Prioritize goals, such as:
      1. Aesthetics for human pleasure;
      2. Single-species benefit;
      3. Multiple-species benefit in ranked order;
      4. Mixed-species integrated and equal benefit;
      5. 'No action,' as part of a scientific baseline study.

Stage Two
1. Discuss the state of our knowledge; decide whether we need additional data, or can make provisional decisions. If we need data, plan for these with a timeline. Project the consequences of no action, and of various actions.
2. Choose goals, strategies, and management plans. Set a date at which to revisit these decisions in the light of new data.

All this takes time, and many of us have to make decisions about our landscapes without the rich information we desire. But no matter how much information we have, creative decisions will be necessary.

Ten

Which Species have the Best Writers?

The Politics of Nature in a Garden

My long transparent feeder, heavy with black oil sunflower seeds, hangs from the rose of sharon just off my deck. Purple and house finches, goldfinches and chickadees, yellow warblers and rose breasted grosbeaks all spend their days fluttering in and out of the hedge to feed. Sometimes a rufos towee drops around, or a cardinal, or a carolina wren.

Aggressive blue jays, like the redwing blackbirds, come crashing in and momentarily frighten all others away. The politics of jaybirds is more serious than it appears through my window: these predators often land on the nest of a different species, and quickly puncture the eggs with their beaks.

Even worse are the predations of cowbirds, which flip the eggs from another species' nest, deposit their own, and let their rivals handle the parenting chores.

High above my feeder a row of maples and cherries provides cover to a range of hungry hawks. Small, quick kestrels perch on a rotten cherry limb and wait with the patience of stone. Huge marsh hawks sail above the leafy crowns, casting their shadows on the grass as if to frighten and flush prey skyward.

Seldom have I seen them succeed — the thick hedge of rose of sharon, laced with the vines of Cherokee roses, affords excellent cover for the songbirds. But the hawks are always hungry, and always working.

Down in the grass, three feet below the feeder, a whole group of mammals competes for spilled sunflower seeds. Squirrels, including a pregnant one, a sort of teenager, and a couple of young adults all hover for the chance to do their bit. Chipmunks tunnel underground so they can pop up, sit on hind legs and nibble at the thick seeds. A vole lives in the vinca, and forays out to scavenge among husks when his stomach moves him. Occasionally a long-tailed field mouse whips by. After dark an elegant gray fox visits the deck, gleaning stray seeds one by one with her delicate, measured intensity.

And there's one more player in this political scene: my neighbor's young brindle cat likes to hide beneath my deck. She stretches on the cool earth in the shade, peering through the hastas like a tiger, dreaming of the four-foot leap she'd like to make, so near and yet so far.

Should I worry about the hawks catching songbirds? It is comforting to think that these species have been fighting it out, each surviving quite well, for longer than humans have walked this earth. While that is true, it may not remain true much longer.

According to John Terborgh in *Where Have All the Birds Gone?*, songbirds are disappearing at the rate of one to two percent a year. The reasons have to do with human activities — burning the rainforests in the tropics where some 250 species spend their winters, and clearing land in North America for farms, subdivisions, highways and shopping malls. Given that context, do the hawks have an unfair advantage? After all, they've been legally protected for 40 years or so. Many local populations, such as ospreys in the neighborhood where I live, have been helped back from the brink of extinction. While humans have prohibited

112

hunting, banned the poisonous DDT, and built nesting platforms across the marshes, the expanded population of ospreys have been busy hunting, mostly fish. Now some biologists suspect the fish supplies are running thin. And other protected hawks and owls, as their numbers expand, take a toll on the songbirds.

There are so many humans that any practices to which we take a liking will have major consequences. Americans spend 2 billion dollars annually on birdseed alone, according to a 2002 industry report. A biologist recently warned that "all the grain dumped on the ground is creating an explosion of rodents."

In the enthusiasm to protect birds, Americans have drafted laws to cover them all, including cowbirds and jays, magpies and gulls. But while those species coexist very well with humans, some of the delicate warblers and other small birds do not.

Is this just evolution in action? Yes and no: yes in the sense that environmental changes give selective advantages to some species rather than others; no in that these changes result directly from humanity's interference. When people crowd the beaches and drop food, gulls and crows follow; along with dogs by day and raccoons and foxes by night, these creatures outcompete the piping plovers, which require open beach to nest and raise young. Of course human actions are part of natural selection, so the "no" above is a qualified one, marking cases where we humans have the impression that we act with free will; this would be in contrast the actions of other animals, which we imagine to be determined by a stream of events. Whether this impression of human freedom is accurate is a separate question from the one discussed here.

Recently, on an island off the coast of Massachusetts, gulls were attacking and killing endangered piping plovers. State wildlife managers resorted to poisoning the gulls, which brought forth a storm of criticism from demonstrators, and some letters in local papers. One person wrote: "once we start down that slippery slope, of killing one species to save another, who knows where we will end?"

But humans have been killing the plovers and encouraging gulls for years, through such beach policies as tolerating unleashed dogs where the plovers nest. If one looked at Massachusetts as a whole in 1988, a third of all the land was covered up — with buildings, parking lots, houses, highways, and so forth. Another third was protected by state parks, greenbelts, conservation trusts, and such, while the final third was rapidly being developed.

This is a dynamic context in which humans are altering nature. While we like to walk on the beach, or sit by the window and watch a feeder, and imagine primordial contests between worthy opponents in a 'balance of nature,' such pictures are often illusions. Some of the contestants have powerful human allies, skewing the results to one side.

In a Massachusetts city the population of free-ranging cats reached striking proportions. Living on the rooftops, raiding garbage cans, catching pigeons, some 40,000 unlicensed, unvaccinated cats roamed free. The mayor, worried about disease, proposed that all cats without collars and tags be picked up. The council agreed, and voted his motion. But citizens rebelled. Letters to the editor spoke for the 'rights of cats.' Mayor and council, fingers to the political wind, rescinded their ordinance. The cats had the vote!

During a recent winter in western Massachusetts, game wardens found the remains of a deer run down and killed by dogs. These weren't hunting dogs, they were pets that followed their owners to the school bus, and stood wagging their friendly tails as the kids disappeared from sight. Then the dogs formed packs and headed for the woods at the edge of town. Jumping a deer from a thicket, they set out in pursuit. The snow was deep, and the deer managed to keep ahead of its tormentors until late afternoon, when the dogs turned back and headed for their separate houses. After a night of rest, food, and frolic with their owners, the dogs met each other again at the bus stop, and traveled in a straight line to the point where they had abandoned the chase in the snow.

The deer had survived one day's running, but now was weakened by exertion and hunger. The dogs picked up the scent and soon ran their prey down.

This pattern was observed by wildlife managers often enough so that they formed a new policy of shooting any dog observed chasing a deer. Some people thought this cruel and unjustified. After all, these dogs were pets.

These examples of competition between species, and between individual animals, seem to fit under the heading 'the politics of nature in a garden.' They have in common that humans have altered the dynamics of competition.

Which species are to be winners, and which losers, in the complicated politics of nature in a garden often depends on which side has the best writers.

Narratives and Metanarratives of Conservation Time

Stories frame human knowledge. They are basic to debates within conservation, for every ecosystem is influenced by stories, and may be seen under a variety of interpretations.

These include temporal frameworks. First, there is the description of current system dynamics; second, there are accounts of how the system evolved over time; and third come projections of what might happen, could happen, ought to happen, to specific places. Thinking about nature in a place means imagining the place over time, and beginning a story.

For a conservation writer, the first task is to describe the region in the present tense, including a species inventory and an account of current system dynamics. This includes human interactions with other species, as well as exchanges of energy through the foodweb between various species. Not all details, nor all relations, can be included in this present tense story. So the writer should select the dynamics that seem most important, and present these vividly.

Once the region in question has been established, the next step is writing a past tense account of how things got the way they are today. Natural histories which downplay social components often seem quintessentially scientific, with their dry, factual tone, and their effaced narrator (a storyteller of whom the reader learns nothing). A natural history often establishes a place's authenticity for the reader. For example, if an ecosystem, like the everglades or Yosemite, can be presented as having a unique history, it may seem a special place deserving protection. The ostensibly objective writing of 'natural' history fundamentally relies on our sneaking in concepts of what's authentic, precious, beautiful, or exotic.

Another conservation effect of natural and social histories involves tales of human destruction — say of the passenger pigeon or the buffalo. When a reader sees that part of an ecosystem has been lost, he or she may be moved to conserve what remains.

The third task a conservation writer faces is cast in the future tense — if X happens, Y will happen also. This is the place for plans and recommendations, for ethical and practical claims.

These three steps, describing a place, recounting its history, proposing its future, are fraught with decision processes for the writer. They are never straightforward factual matters, though they rest upon facts; as in all important matters, selection is involved. As William James said, there is always some interest involved whenever facts are stated. I turn now to the interests writers bring when they specify the temporal boundaries of an ecosystem. These are often key to debates, for they attempt to seize the discussion at the outset by specifying which time frames are legitimate and appropriate.

Eleven

How Writers Impose Time upon Nature

Any perspective on an ecosystem requires one to consider the passage of time, and the dynamic interactions of species over temporal intervals. Each element or member of the system has its short-term goals, needs, and interests. For example, the finches' need for seeds and buds, and longer-term interests as well, e.g., the finches' need to have many plants and trees succeed in order to provide cover and food in future years. The plants in turn may depend upon a healthy finch population to swallow and spread their seeds. One can come into this system at any point and begin to tell its stories. But how does one know which are true, and which cultural projections?

As ecologists observe, they attempt to verify and especially to falsify hypotheses. But of course they can only test one of infinitely many possible hypotheses. Complete knowledge of an ecosystem is quite impossible.

These questions arise within larger temporal frameworks, which direct the focus and methods of conservationists. Raglon and Scholtmeijer have argued that metanarratives, often unconscious yet pervasive, control narratives. For example, all of nature writing, from Columbus to Lopez, assumes the situation of the writer's mind staring out at nature, describing, comparing, evaluating. This dualism, subject 'subjugating' object, ultimately drains meaning from the object, reduces nature to a mere presentation, a lifeless other. Echoes of this original situation arise in metaphysical behaviorism, in which writers deny other minds because they aren't directly presented, and in the general attitude that developing nature for profit violates no ethical rules because nature is material substance — not a community of living, intrinsically valuable, subjects.

Raglon and Scholtmeijer suggest addressing the subject/object metanarrative of nature writing through postmodern textual strategies. In different ways, these call attention to the writer's presence, and break the illusion of invisible, authoritative eyes (the authorial I) appropriating nature as resources.

Applying this kind of analysis to the temporal dimension of ecosystems, consider three 'invisible' metanarratives — cultural time frames that often structure environmental debates:

(1) Discounting. This is the economic planning method used to determine whether a project is feasible. Assuming an inflation ('discount') rate of 5%, one dollar today will be worth $.95 a year from today. If I have $100 million tied up in whaling ships I must decide whether to harvest whales at a sustainable level, or kill them all in one year. On the former strategy I may not make enough profit to equal what I could make in, say, blue chip stocks. On the latter strategy, I reap enormous profits this year, sell the ships, and roll all the money over into stocks or safe bonds.

The economist John Kenneth Galbraith and others have pointed out that CEOs and corporate boards have a limited perspective by which to measure success. Most CEOs keep a job for only a few years, and so their careers will be measured by increments of 4-5 years in their companies' histories. Hence a rational CEO would not naturally be thinking about the long-term health of her corporation, in making investment decisions. The destruction and/or restoration of ecosystems which result from such decisions would take decades to unfold, and thus would not easily be measured by two to three year ecological studies.

Time frames dictated by discounting or "net present value analysis" often control decisions which affect species health or even survival; think of disappearing Atlantic bluefin tuna, elephants and rhinos, rain forests and old growth forests. In the Pacific Northwest some towns dependent on logging old growth forests have demanded they be allowed to continue, in the name of their jobs. On the other side, conservationists have pointed out that the old growth forests in question would be logged out in 5 to 10 years, and the town would die anyway. Why, they asked, should this resource be destroyed to delay the inevitable pain of relocation and retraining for workers?

This kind of debate is ultimately structured by the metanarrative of the lumber company's discounting analysis. In order to 'justify' investment in logging and milling equipment which 'harvests' the forests with incredible speed, the trees 'must' be cut at a rapid rate. This ensures the death of both trees and jobs. By cutting back on the rate of harvest, both forest and jobs could be preserved indefinitely. But such decisions are made by MBAs in air-conditioned offices in cities, far from the communities and habitats at stake.

(2) Ecologists' Budgets. Most ecological field studies are funded for only a few years at most. Data on long-term trends, and verification of relationships — like that between ozone depletion and vanishing amphibians — are sometimes painfully lacking. While many suspect that frogs are disappearing due to ultraviolet-caused skin cancers, and songbird populations are declining due to rain forest burning and wetland draining, stronger data are needed. Multiple causes make it difficult to tease out the statistical significance of any one. For example, amphibians also suffer from a widespread and fatal virus, and birds are beginning to

die from H5N1, the avian influenza.

Thus, threats to nature are sometimes difficult to substantiate in court. Destruction of New England forests by acid rain from Midwestern coal-fired plants is a classic case in point. Because of the time frames of research project funding — their less visible metanarratives — ecological arguments are often weaker than they might be.

(3) Development Pressure. Partly because of the expanding frontier heritage in America, many believe that people have a right to develop private land regardless of the common good. Neither private nor public actors have enough money to buy all the land needed (Fairfax, et al.). Short of outright ownership, how can citizens meet conservation goals?

Many environmental debates concern rates of habitat loss. A conservationist looks at the rate of change in a region, and asks what kinds of constraints are possible. The Endangered Species Act provided one of the best tools in this regard, and the degree to which it often comes under attack testifies to its power and effectiveness. But it offers a kind of sad, minimal focus on the problem of disappearing nature, not a vision of increase and security for diverse species. Planners must play catch-up, and their theme must be growth management. But why should their best game be management of an 'inevitable' social and political trend? Only because they have accepted the development metanarrative that structures debates over zoning, watershed protection, and a host of community issues.

Discount rates, ecologists' budgets, and development pressures are three ways in which cultural time frames structure environmental debates. They set the terms of debate for particular environmental struggles. Such ways of thinking seem to bind nature and society into a single temporal whole, and they constrain the possible understandings, arguments, and protection plans one can imagine. Around particular debates, these time boundaries seem to create a world.

Time as Epic History

When we think of cultural time we remember that each culture has its memories by which to measure history. Each has unique temporal landmarks dividing the year. Generally these are great founding events, which bestow cosmic significance on a society or state, and spiritual significance on its patriotic and faithful members. Each culture has its golden age, toward which it looks for guidance, and from which it measures how far it has fallen. For the U.S.A. the golden age remains that pristine moment when European eyes first touched the New World shores. Environmentalists are sometimes tempted by a version of a founding event, cast in terms of a scientific-sounding epic.

The biologist Edward O. Wilson has called the great story of evolution the epic of our age. An epic is a work of art, a story or narrative, constructed to inspire respect for its protagonists, its heroes and villains. Wilson hopes this one can give us a vision of our origins, an awestruck appreciation of beauty, and a basis for ethically cherishing all life on the planet. This is a creative and attractive idea. It takes all the countless dramas of nature past, all the contingent events that have birthed one species and ended another, and combines them into a single grand tale. That tale is one of increasing complexity, feeling, reason, beauty, and morality. Of course "increasing complexity" does not mean there is a progressive plan at work, at least not according to Darwin. This is a point of which Stephen Jay Gould was fond of reminding us. There is nothing 'better' about a brown hare than a white hare, they just fit different niches. Similarly, a dodo was more complex than a roach, but not better, nor even better adapted. It's tempting to project the sequences we approve, and anoint as "progressive," backwards, and attribute to nature the story which, after all, produced ourselves. This move is not scientific, but it does seem to fit with the notion of an epic, which is a literary form, a dramatist's creation.

Wilson's metaphor identifies 'evolution,' as a pattern

of facts, with 'epic,' a product of culture. The vision is a conceptual feat, presented in acts of writing, which carries the power to move us toward greater concern for nature, and greater restraint of development. It is affecting partly because it plays upon the dual sense of humans as living within the epic (products of a single great evolutionary process) and outside it — able to revise the ending.

Wilson's concept may lead some people to confuse the contingency of nature with the design of a written epic. The story of evolution is a description of events which might have happened differently; dinosaurs might have survived those meteor-caused dust clouds, and as a result mammals might never have possessed a niche into which humans eventually emerged. Even more drastically, Earth might have lost its atmosphere, as Mars did. Every past event, from the big bang (or great radiance) some 13 billion years ago, to Cro-Magnons outcompeting Neanderthals, to the survival of my own ancestors in the American Revolution, are part of my story. And a beautiful epic it is — to me — since it 'leads' up to this moment, in which I have the pleasure of breathing, drinking coffee, and writing this line. But to speak of the history of nature is to invoke a great series of contingent events; they were not logically determined, nor fated, and might have been otherwise.

On the other hand when one writes (or speaks an epic, as in ancient Greece), the author's intentions control the narrative structure. The writer often knows the ending before crafting the opening line. Time frames, like other aspects of stories, reveal intentionality and design. Before science, people everywhere believed they lived in a world designed and influenced on a continuing basis by minds or spirits. Whether they thought of this in terms of a multiplicity or a monotheism was a secondary detail.

But with science was born the idea of an open ending — a collection of stories or hypotheses to be tested, never embraced blindly. This enabled the separation of teleological

122

stories (the beginning happens for the sake of the end) from open or scientific ones.

All this leads to the recognition that nature is a great mystery, lying beyond our theories and hopes, beyond all our projections. Different stories will seem to fit the world, according to the observations we make. This is true in the sciences, such as biology and ecology, and equally true in conservation work. Before discussion can begin, we must create a slice of time, a frame of reference.

Creating the Time of Local Nature

Whether one constructs and tests hypotheses within evolutionary theory, creates artful narratives, or conducts a species inventory as prelude to crafting a protection plan, one must project an umbrella of cultural time. A plan for a site cannot be founded on natural time frames alone, but must depend upon cultural ones as well. This is not a disaster, and does not open the door to exploitation of nature through the claim that all protection plans are subjective and relative.

In order to describe an ecosystem at issue in a particular case, and to proceed from there toward a protection plan, bridges must be built between author and audience. A writer must begin somewhere, with the equivalent of a golden age claim, or a mythic statement like "In the beginning the people came from the west..." For example in a town planning process the writer might say, "The natural values in this town include..." and proceed to list species, ecosystems, and landscape views. Such statements establish that several generations of people have cherished the land, and that their legacy is now the current generation's mission to protect. Within a comprehensive town planning process such statements are first offered by individuals in small, 'brainstorming' groups, and eventually make their way into community plans which are ratified by a vote. At that point they take on legal status, becoming a kind of constitution for the protection of local places. Note that such statements have no ultimate warrant, no foundational philosophic basis, but are records of cultural patterns of valuing nature. They derive authority from their performance in the writing, from their acceptance by a community, and sometimes by inclusion within a deed. In this sense they aren't that different from claims made in documents like the US constitution, which in some way represent cultural patterns, and are subject to similar quandaries of interpretation.

Garden and Wilderness

What differences exist between the garden metaphor, with its requirement of social details and temporal frameworks, and a wilderness metaphor? I suggest that this is most importantly a historical question. It's a matter of how we interpret nature over a stretch of time.

I defined a garden as an ecosystem which has been, and continues to be, significantly influenced by human activities. It turns out a wilderness also fits this definition. Vine Deloria, Jr., has said that before the white man arrived there was no wilderness. His point is that native tribes regarded sections of the landscape as their homes, and managed them accordingly. Whites redefined these areas and their owners as 'wild,' and proceeded to destroy both. Later, with the natives removed, whites discovered the need to preserve remnants of the 'wild' lands.

Recent research suggests that prior to 1492 the Americas may have been home to as many as 100 million native people. Every major watershed was 'found' by Europeans to contain open grasslands, which seem to have been maintained by the intentional use of fire. 'Primeval wilderness' — old growth forests instead of grasslands — may have followed European settlement in many areas, more than preceded it. In any case the arguments are historical ones. They cannot be settled by introspection, nor in standing rapt before a towering woods, and noting the differences between this and perennial beds.

When we designate a wilderness area we imagine ourselves preserving objective nature, all its species bound in a common time stretching back to our golden age, the moment our European predecessors touched the New World. Those newcomers practiced ethnic cleansing, large mammal extinction, and reduction of biological diversity in favor of monocultural cropping. For thousands of years before that, native peoples altered the landscape through fire, and probably drove many large mammals to extinction. In well-documented cases they also invaded and destroyed their neighbors.

Coming late into this complex, post-imperial landscape, like gardeners the world over we have cleared and planted, crafted and applied our cultural notions of beauty and rightness. Having defined ourselves as protectors of the primal landscape, the American Eden, we are now conserving ourselves. This is surprising, but not offensive or wrong. It is simply the truth about how we approach our habitats, our landscapes.

Conservation visions and appeals must begin and end with stories casting the species that interest us, and we ourselves, into a time frame our audiences will consider as a realm for discussion and argument. Rich descriptions of natural events, detailed natural histories, and projected images of restrained social interactions with ecosystems can raise the critical mass of votes to protect specific places. This is the work of conservation writers.

Twelve

Two Interpretations of Leopold's Land Ethic

The Appealing Idea of a Land Ethic

For many people, Aldo Leopold's *A Sand County Almanac*, published in 1949, captures the spirit of contemporary conservation like no other book. Part One reports wildlife events and seasonal changes on the abused Wisconsin farm which Leopold and his family lovingly restored. Through rich, invitational descriptions and elegantly compressed sentences, Leopold brings his reader to picture a skunk making its way across January snow, to hear the music of cranes circling an ancient marsh, and to smell the sawdust of a lightning-felled oak as the sawyer slowly renders it into firewood. Part I reveals the power of a fine nature writer to make his reader love a particular landscape. His techniques are those of the storyteller, and the detective of nature — unfolding secrets of woodcock and rabbit, of maple and pine.

By the time the reader arrives at Part Two, enough hints have been given about the Leopold family so that one identifies with their weekend trips to the farm, their efforts to restore 'the shack' as well as their fields. The reader deems it right not only that Leopold should protect wild nature there, but that he and his family should find a niche as well. One respects Leopold's textual imagining of his chosen place, his deeds of preservation, and also the 'fit' between his family and the land.

Leopold has gradually brought us inside his ethical concerns, such as whether he should shoot more than a single woodcock on an afternoon's hunt; he has presented us with private aesthetic questions, including whether he should chop a maple sapling or a pine. They are stealing each other's sunlight and soil, and one or the other should go. Otherwise, each will have a stunted life, unlovely to look at, with lost possibilities for fulfillment, even perhaps for reproduction.

In Part Two, Leopold draws upon his expertise as a wildlife manager to tell bitter stories of the human destruction of other species. Passenger pigeon and buffalo, prairie chicken and bear, and countless other creatures once roamed the Wisconsin woods and countryside. Through his natural and social histories, Leopold portrays a wasteful frontier mentality and culture. Rhetorically, he builds shared values (between reader and writer), and introduces new information, a broad perspective on environmental history.

These stories aren't all narrated in an impersonal voice; the most compelling among them confesses his own youthful shooting of a wolf mother, and the transforming moment when he watched the 'fierce green fire' in her eyes die. His own act of killing her became a symbol for him of a disrespectful culture of nature. And by revealing that memory he draws us toward his new persona, or self projected into his text. Before the killing he was simply a man of his time, shooting 'varmints' or 'predators' on sight. But afterward he was haunted by her life, her intelligence, wasted on the mountainside for a man's momentary diversion. Something was wrong with that man and with his culture.

Part Three, 'The Upshot,' reaches a greater level of generality in its discussion of conservation problems. Here Leopold introduces the idea of a land ethic — as an extension of the gradual ethical progress which moved from Greek to Barbarian, male to female, slave to freeperson, adult to child. It is time, he suggests, to extend our ethical concern to the biotic community (which is what he means by 'land').

This idea strikes many people today as an exciting one. The phrase 'land ethic' seems just right to capture a certain quality of conscience, a spiritual state which one might call the will to preserve. It might be contrasted with what one might call the will to develop (in the sense of converting ecosystems into profit centers).

Aldo Leopold has inspired conservationists for over 50 years, and there is a growing sense of urgency that the land ethic idea should catch on with a wider public and enter general education. In what follows, I consider the first of two very different interpretations of the concept which Leopold offered; later I present the second of these, which I believe is often more useful for conservation writers. The first attempts to base ethical claims on 'the truth about the world' — independently of human beings; the second takes a more modest position, and approaches conservation work as a cousin of historic preservation. Each interpretation offers a path to communication with audiences with the power to protect land.

Two Approaches to the Land Ethic

Leopold says, "In short, a land ethic changes the role of *Homo sapiens* from conqueror of the land-community to plain member and citizen of it. It implies respect for his fellow-members, and also respect for the community as such" (204).

This passage, along with others which assert that soils, waters, plants, and animals have a "right to continued existence" (in the passage preceding the quote above), have led many conservationists to identify the possibility of a land ethic, or even any sort of environmental ethic, with an affirmation that nature contains intrinsic value.

This language has begun to appear in environmental protection documents. For example, the 1995 Minnesota Department of Natural Resources management plan for Lake Superior specifies protecting the "intrinsic value" of the "resource." This is interesting because in traditional usage resources have extrinsic, not intrinsic, value — they are for somebody's use. So two different philosophical languages collide in this practical text.

This is much like references to 'human rights' in treaties. That is, no one expects the authors of management plans or treaties to explain their terms in a philosophical sense; the words have an operational meaning, which is to say that all parties know what must be done. Still, philosophers and others should explore such language, chart its relations with other expressions, and examine its connotations and denotations.

The appearance of "intrinsic value" or "resource" in conservation documents could be considered an instance of trickle down, from more intellectual discussions. In other words, some philosophers might argue for a literal, denotative reference for the phrase "intrinsic value," and as a result this expression might gradually slip into common usage. (Something like this must have happened with the phrase "human rights.") But when a phrase like "intrinsic value" is used by those unschooled in technical philosophy, in a context like that of the Lake Superior plan, it has a different use. It is suggestive of some kind of value for the lake independent of human valuers, but vague as to exactly what this means.

One approach to conservation writing which Leopold endorses in Part Three of Sand County tries to clarify, use and argue for expressions like "the intrinsic value of the lake." But the other approach, which he also endorses, appeals instead to what a place like Lake Superior has meant to decades of people living on its shores. As a part of their history, it contributes to their cultural identities. This is what Leopold means by stressing the cultural or "split rail" value of nature. He chooses this phrase because the image of a split rail fence is loaded with nostalgic American associations, including an image of Abraham Lincoln splitting rails in frontier Illinois. Anything which reminds Americans of an ideal past (such as a frontier wilderness near cabin and fence) will help persuade them to conservation action now (to preserve the remnants of that historic and even patriotic wilderness).

Brian G. Norton (1996) has argued that Leopold believed the language of the intrinsic value of nature, as well as the language of the cultural value of nature, offered useful ways of communicating with the public about conservation goals. Which language, and conceptual scheme, is superior? Norton says Leopold considered this undecidable by appeals to facts. In other words, each path offers a comprehensive way of thinking and talking about nature. Each approach is logically compatible with every fact, or description of fact. If this is so, it means that the question of intrinsic value is not a matter of factual knowledge, but rather a way of organizing such knowledge. "Intrinsic" and "extrinsic" are words applied to conceptual schemes, rather than to elements of nature, such as bluebirds and bears. A bluebird can be a certain shade of blue, and fly at a certain speed, but it cannot have a quality called "intrinsic value" in the same sense. In the early years of the 20th Century, the English philosopher G.E. Moore claimed that we have intuitions of goodness; we actually sense a property which he called "the good," and which exists objectively like blue or square. This position has been thoroughly discussed, (e.g. by McIntyre and by Johnson), and it would be rare today to find anyone who defends it within traditional ethics. Philosophers recognize that people often feel strongly that a particular action is objectively good, but they attempt to give an account of this feeling in some other way than positing Moore's intuited property. That position seems to require an outdated theory of language, which treats words like "good" as names;

starting from that point, there must be an object for them to name. By analogy, some philosophers attempt to account for our sense that a state of nature is a good one, by arguing for an objective property which "grounds" the judgment; but, as in the case of Moore's theory, few would maintain that this property can be directly sensed or intuited. Most feel there must be another way to account for our descriptions and evaluations of nature.

The trouble is, when one constructs a sophisticated theory of language which seems to explain the commonsense notion of goodness, and to account for our folk psychology sense of objective goodness, some people may feel it just doesn't account for their experience. And in discussing a land ethic, people who love nature, and have an intuitive will to preserve it, often feel that anything less than affirmation of its objective, intrinsic value simply fails to do justice to commonsense and to folk psychology. Let's discuss these concepts for a moment before returning to intrinsic v. extrinsic value.

Commonsense and Theory

Science slowly and painfully made us aware that the earth is round and circles the sun, natural selection shapes species, motion is relative to an observer's position, the brain produces the mind, and the universe grew from a spec 13 billion years ago. To some isolated people the earth still seems flat, and the sun appears to circle overhead; to large numbers of people species seem created by God; most of us don't believe motion and time are relative at the scale of ordinary experience; to many people the mind appears to exist independently of the brain, and they believe it will survive the brain; and every day one hears skeptical views of the big bang — partly because it's so counterintuitive. So, even if someone presented us with a convincing analysis of our normal feelings about the intrinsic value of nature, explaining these feelings in terms of conceptual confusions and psychological projections, we might angrily reject it and strike the messenger from our guest list.

This problem, that science and philosophy sometimes rattle our commonsense worldview, has no general solution. It's not enough to say that with education comes willingness to accept evidence of unseen entities and causes, and a weakening of folk psychology. The answer is not that commonsense is wrong, and science and philosophy right, because those disciplines must always return to commonsense as a baseline of understanding. On the other hand, commonsense is frequently composed of outdated, discredited theories, like our 'sense' that the sun circles the earth (Papineau 20). New theories with a claim on our attention must explain why commonsense is wrong, or right, in every case. Commonsense embodies and asserts the world we are born into, and into which we bring children. Sometimes people embrace an extreme theory of unseen forces, such as classical Marxism, Freudian psychology, a Jungian Collective Unconscious, or a metaphysical behaviorism which denies the existence of minds because they can't be observed. I choose these examples because many people alive today have embraced them at one time, but now find the invisible entities and forces of these theories, and the lax rules of evidence which they require, a bit embarrassing. Just as science must always attempt better theories to explain our common, baseline experience, so philosophy must continually attempt better analyses of theories, and beliefs, but always contrast these analyses with the commonsense world they are meant to explain. Maybe one day we'll have better theories. That's just the way things are.

Leopold's Paths

If we consider Leopold's two paths to conservation, one through objective value in nature, and the other through split-rail cultural value, how do we choose? If either way of speaking is consistent with all the facts we know, and is capable of presenting those facts, then these ways of speaking are not factual claims themselves. They are conceptual ones. They are frameworks or schemes for organizing facts. In such a situation, how does one choose between conceptual schemes?

One might think of descriptions of facts as part of an object-language, a concrete language I'll call Level 1. Here we'll find descriptions like "this air after rain is clear and sweet," and also general statements like "foxes are scarce this year." These are statements which can be supported, or discounted, through observations.

Level 2 is more abstract, and we could call it a metalanguage. It will contain claims like "a fox has intrinsic value" or "foxes have (extrinsic) cultural value for my community, because on an unconscious level they remind us of the wilderness period in American history." These statements cannot be verified by observations. Rather, they serve to organize Level 1 observations and theories. How does one choose between conflicting Level 2 claims?

By turning to Level 3, a second-order metalanguage (or language about the metalanguage), we find criteria for deciding between competing Level 2 claims. For example we may ask: Which conceptual scheme is more elegant? (This often means: Which is simpler?) Or we might ask: Which scheme leads to more effective conservation? (I have argued it is inappropriate to begin with the conclusions we desire, such as "protect this place," and work backwards to first-order claims we think will help, like "nature is holy." But pragmatic third-order claims like "using the intrinsic value language in the Lake Superior management plan will increase public support for conservation" are different. They may be true as first-order claims about persuasion, without asserting anything at all about nature.)

Norton argues that Leopold held just such a sophisticated view of language (though he didn't express it exactly this way). While Leopold leaned *emotionally* toward the intrinsic value way of speaking, he believed this would never persuade hard-nosed developer types. Therefore, as a strategic matter, Leopold favored appeals to cultural value in conservation writing. I agree with Norton about Leopold's view, and with Leopold about strategies for conservation writing. (The original title for *A Sand County Almanac* was *Great Possessions.* When Leopold died, leaving the manuscript under contract with a publisher, the title was changed to avoid confusion with the Dickens novel *Great Expectations.* This change seems a good idea; the original title also suggests that Leopold gave significant weight to the 'extrinsic' way of speaking.)

Still, many conservationists disagree with this perspective, and push hard for the embrace of intrinsic value. They do this not only for the sake of public discourse, but because they have religious feelings about nature. They often argue that unless nature is cherished intrinsically, conservation will ultimately fail. In the following essay I summarize some recent work on the philosophical issues at stake.

Thirteen

Philosophy and the Value of Nature

Intrinsic Value in Nature

The assertion that nature has intrinsic value can seem obvious; after all, who doesn't acknowledge the intrinsic value of a bluebird, or of a mountain lion? They needn't be good *for* something, in order to be valuable in themselves.

The intrinsic value idea expresses commonsense. But note that it's a recent kind of commonsense. Bluebirds were once too common to value highly, and mountain lions were enemies in pioneer days. The scarcity of these species has led to a changing of commonsense.

We have an odd situation: "the intrinsic value of nature" sounds like a matter of objective truth, while acts of valuing particular creatures like bluebirds and lions seem subjective in some way. Claims about people valuing bluebirds and lions are historical ones, events the emergence of which could be dated. While "the intrinsic" sounds culture-free and absolute, "the extrinsic" seems culture-bound and relative.

In the early 1970s philosophers began to discuss the concept of an environmental ethic, and to ask what the extension of traditional ethical positions to the biotic community might mean. Are environmental problems just a new class of cases for analysis by theories like utilitarianism, social-contractarianism, deontologism, and intuitionism? Or in rethinking the human-land community relationship, are new models and concepts needed?

By the 1980s intense philosophical debates had begun over intrinsic value, inherent value, scarcity, animal rights, and ecosystem rights. While many issues have been clarified, the debates seem interminable. Leaders in the field still pass each other in the night, using different definitions of key terms, and express anger at each other over misunderstandings. In short, environmental ethics has arrived at the gridlock which has long characterized ethics in general.

This is a shame, because the work of philosophers could clarify the language and arguments in question, and aid rather than provoke conservationists. Yet the sheer weight of technicality, the multi-year literature of arguments challenging anyone who would become current, and the compressed nature of much philosophical writing, all separate academic discussion from grassroots conservation. Philosophers continually refine their theories, as they should, with conservationists left to their best rhetorical devices.

I will argue that both kinds of language, of intrinsic and extrinsic value, have important roles in conservation. The writer's goal is conservation action, which usually requires the consensus of an intellectually diverse group. Even if the reader disagrees with me, what follows will help writers avoid ambiguities, with their consequent fallacies of equivocation.

John O'Neill, writing in The Monist, has distinguished three different senses of "intrinsic value" which are sometimes meant:

(1) Intrinsic value can mean non-instrumental value. Some values are ends-in-themselves, others are means to those ends. Not all values can be instrumental, O'Neill says,

on pain of infinite regress. Now, for an environmental ethic to make sense, it must name natural values which are not mere instruments, but which are worthwhile for their own sake. Recognizing these values might be what Leopold meant in the passage mentioned earlier, when he spoke of "respect for (man's) fellow members, and also respect for the community as such."

So far so good. But questions arise when someone makes the claim, as Kant did, that only human beings can be ends-in-themselves. Why should this be so? Why shouldn't my daughter's rabbit also be recognized as an end-in-itself? In order to answer this question, environmental ethicists sometimes claim that "intrinsic value" denotes something independent of human valuers.

(2) Intrinsic value can mean value possessed by an object solely in virtue of its intrinsic properties. O'Neill offers a distinction with regard to these: Can they be characterized without regard to human beings? Take my daughter's rabbit. It has interests which can be called "good of" it, such as health and peace. Though humans are required for these goods to be recognized, the goods exist independently of humans. Their description requires no reference to humans. This sense of independent existence may support the idea that non-humans are sometimes ends-in-themselves.

O'Neill also says that:

(3) Sometimes "intrinsic value" substitutes for "objective value," indicating value existing independently of the valuations of valuers. For example, the rabbit's good might be a value independent of human valuers, but not independent of the rabbit's own valuations. But can rabbits be valuers? They have goods, and no doubt are aware of some of them (in the sense that internal states of hunger and desire for a lettuce leaf may accompany a rabbit's raid on a garden). But as one considers simpler organisms, such internal states become more problematic and controversial. Still, does awareness ever matter for the existence of values?

Do maples and pines have goods? If so, can trees be called valuers? Not without stretching the term. But since trees do have goods, perhaps the term needs to be stretched.

O'Neill argues that anything with a life can be characterized as having things which are goods of them, and since these values can be characterized without reference to actual or possible humans, then there is intrinsic value in the sense of objective value. In this he follows von Wright (1963), with whom he disagrees about one very troublesome case, that of collective entities.

This sounds abstract, even definitional, but it involves a very important point for environmental ethics: what is good for an ecosystem can be bad for the individual organisms within. Collectives (like bioregions, but also like bureaucracies, nations, unions, and families) are not literally alive, yet they have goods; sometimes the conditions that cause a nation to flourish can cause individuals within to suffer and die. In the case of a species, it can be too successful, reaching the stages of population growth which ecologists call overshoot, crash and die-off. To avoid this, and for the sake of species health, many individuals must perish without reproducing.

O'Neill says the class of beings that can have objective goods is identical with the class of beings that can (non-metaphorically) flourish. And the class of living beings is a subset of this last class.

At this point my reader's eyes may be glazing over, and he or she may be thinking "philosophy is all definitions anyway." But wait: some of the most difficult questions in formulating a land ethic, especially if it is to aid a management plan for an actual place, turn on whether individuals should be sacrificed for the sake of collectives.

Should deer be killed to protect forests? Should gulls be killed to safeguard a scarce species like piping plovers? Forests and piping plover species are collective entities; targeted deer and gulls are individual organisms. These questions are unavoidable. Let's examine another point O'Neill brings up about (3) above.

Subjects and Objects of Valuations

It's possible to hold that valuers are all human subjects (call this 'subjectivism' or S); nevertheless some objects of value are non-human (for example a rabbit's health). One mustn't confuse the sources of value judgments with the objects which those judgments include. Thus a philosopher like Baird Callicott can follow David Hume in subjectivism, yet argue for 'intrinsic value in nature.'

On the other hand, one could also hold that some values, such as healthy states of trees or ecosystems, are non-human, and do not depend for their existence upon human judgments (call this 'objectivism' or O). Yet, partisans of O might oppose such values if they are harmful to humans (the AIDS virus, for example). Just because a value exists, why should humans support and protect it?

Position S, then, can be subjectivist yet embrace biocentric goods, or goods which don't involve humans; position O can be objectivist yet somewhat anthropocentric, meaning that humans might recognize natural values but deny obligations to care for them when they threaten us. These alternatives are not always evident to debaters, who sometimes cast these forms of S or O as either necessary, or deal-breakers, for the very possibility of environmental ethics.

S and O represent not moral theories (about what one ought to do), nor ethical theories (about justifications for moral theories), but theories about ethics. They model the ways ethical judgments come about, not what their content should be. (In terms of the above discussion of Norton on Leopold, moral claims like "protect endangered species" occur at an analogue of Level 1, ethical claims like "protect endangered species because they have goods of themselves," occur at Level 2, and metaethical claims like "ethical claims are all based on human valuers" occur at Level 3.)

Metaethical theories are logically independent of ethical theories. O'Neill points out that this is well known in ethics generally, but tends to be forgotten in the heat of environmental debate. The reason for this forgetting is that it is standard to argue that possession of moral goods entails moral considerability. "Moral standing or considerability belongs to whatever has a good of its own," says Paul Taylor in his book, Should Trees Have Standing?

But this is false, O'Neill argues. Just because AIDS or a dictatorship have objective goods does not entail obligations to promote them. "...there is a logical gap between facts and oughts. 'Y is good' does not entail 'Y ought to be realized.'"

Conclusions

O'Neill succeeds in clarifying several reasonable senses in which one can say nature has intrinsic value. He also shows how the subjectivism/objectivism debate is irrelevant to practical questions about a land ethic, because these are third-level metaethical theories about the sources of ethical judgments, not first-level moral claims about which values should be protected, nor second-level claims about why particular moral theories are appropriate.

In having a clear way of expressing that ends-in-themselves exist throughout nature, we seem near to reaching a land ethic. Yet, having followed O'Neill, it's as if we're looking at nature across a river, unable to decide which of many values to support. We can see the trees, but cannot derive from their intrinsic value an obligation to protect them.

He suggest two possible bridges:

(1) One might invoke a general moral claim linking objective values with obligations to promote them, such as an objectivist version of utilitarianism, e.g., "we have a duty to maximize the total moral good in the world." But

this path has problems: How are goods to be compared? How are qualitatively different goods to be weighed? And how do we avoid 'goods' like the pleasures of sadists? O'Neill is not sanguine that any such general program can overcome the logical gap at issue. Of course these problems with utilitarianism arise in conjunction with any ethical discussion, not just biotic issues. And their seriousness in undermining utility as the sole criterion of value does not prevent us from occasionally having a useful debate about ecosystem management. We might discuss, for example, the relative merits of using fire to manage a particular ecosystem, framed in terms of the utility or pleasure and pain of all the organisms affected.

(2) He is far more enthusiastic about an Aristotelian approach, which would have us look at the goals of any activity in order to grasp the kinds of practices, or excellences, required for success. In order for us to flourish, we must care for our friends. The best human life requires friendship, which entails concern for friends without calculation of specific benefits to oneself. The 'excellence' of personal flourishing requires an 'excellence' in practicing friendship. And this requires a degree of unselfishness. Perhaps our understanding of this can provide an analogy for friendship with nature.

I have called the impulse toward conservation the "will to preserve," and it may be a condition of the best human life, especially in a world as environmentally threatened as our own. But this kind of friendship toward nature must pervade a person.

This sounds grand, but in actual friendships isn't there some element of self interest, as there is in our dependency on nature? The friendship analogy is worth exploring. Several philosophers have attempted to explain friendship, but each account seems to settle on relationships in particular circumstances; there is no consensus about a general meaning of the term "friend."

According to Mark Vernon, in his book *The Philosophy of Friendship*, Plato offers a useful account. Socrates, as represented by Plato, was constantly trying to make friends.

> ...the value of the Platonic conception of friendship is that it is open ended: there is always more to discover and enjoy in the best friendships. Friendship is a way of life, in the sense of being a constant process of becoming with others. It is distinguished from other kinds of love by a dynamic that results in an increasing self-awareness coupled to knowing the other better. Friends want to know each other and be known (32).

In considering analogies between our relations with nature and with friends, we should recognize varieties of friendship. But we needn't be tied to concepts of friendships we've known in the past. As our discussion of commonsense and theory showed, there are times when new theories improve commonsense. Thus we might pick and choose from various models of friendship, until we create one that seems to fit our desired relations with nature, and that offers the conceptual bridge needed for a land ethic.

Vernon focuses on increasing self-awareness coupled with knowing the other better. This is surely the experience of everyone who knows a friend well, and of everyone who knows a natural place over time. We have discussed how many species are still discovered each year, and how mysterious are the dynamics of ecosystems. Cast our investigative grid as we will, specifying grain and extent, and we find secrets at every scale. Talk to residents of a landscape, and we learn the most unexpected facts about fauna and flora. What we don't know about nature is like what we don't know about our good friends — there is always more to know. As boys in the woods, my friends and I discovered that each day brought surprises. Once two whitetail does followed two bobcats. Another day a buzzard laid its heavy egg on the ground inside a cavernous oak. As we learned the strange ways of animals, we learned about each other, and ourselves.

After a boyhood in the forest, cherishing those friends and still being surprised by them today, the analogy between nature and friendship seems a natural one to me. It surely does to others who had the blessing of an outdoor life. But as the world's cities grow, populations expand; each day fewer people can have sustained adventures in natural places. When tomorrow's citizens look across the conceptual river at wild beings, ends-in-themselves, and think of the strange creatures over there, which ones will they support? What kind of bridges will these people construct? What will lead them to care about the panther or the rattlesnake? Will some form of friendship analogy have appeal?

In the opening essay, "River of Silence," I told the story of the canoe trip where I had to promise not to reveal fragile places along the river. Philosopher Bonnelle Strickling noted that this introduces an important metaphor for the whole project of the book: our relation to the natural world is a kind of maternal preservation, analogous to the treatment of someone who has been abused and wounded. "The difference would be," Bonnie said, "that this protection needs to be continuous."

Both maternal and paternal roles require watchful silence, as an element of protecting the vulnerable. Like friendship, parenting may offer metaphors by which we can cross the conceptual river in support of wild interests.

O'Neill, drawing from Aristotle, and Vernon, drawing from Plato, highlight elements of friendship which may be useful to conservation writers. For Aristotle, friendship like other practices has its own excellence, its own virtue; it is both unselfish and self-satisfying. In this light, through caring for wild creatures we may find personal

145

rewards. Socrates modeled a social life in which the search for knowledge required endless questioning of his friends. This parallels the way ecological science, focused on other species, returns to us medicines and knowledge of our own history and behavior.

We are not exactly Aristotelian friends, nor Socratic friends, nor parents in our efforts to understand and appreciate animals and plants. Despite our wish to know them, they remain citizens of another country. Yet these varieties of friendship are rich material for encouraging conservation. Storytellers will raise the bridges.

Bibliography

Allen, Timothy F.H. and Hoekstra, Thomas W., T*oward a Unified Ecology,* NY: Columbia University Press 1993.

Allende, Isabella, *Eva Luna*, NY: Knopf 1988.

Alverson, William, S., Walter Kuhlmann, and Donald M. Waller, *Wild Forests: Conservation Biology and Public Policy.* Chicago: Island Press 1994.

Bluestone, James, *Three Affiliated Tribes Program of Economic Recovery from the Impact of the Garrison Dam,* Master of Regional Planning thesis, University of Massachusetts Amherst, 1986.

Buttimer, Anne and Wallin, Luke, *Nature and Identity in Cross-cultural Perspective*, Boston: Kluwer Academic Publishers, 1999.

Carlson, Janet, et al., "Another UMD History," student essay, University of Massachusetts, Dartmouth, for Professor Wallin, 1991.

Carroll, Tracy, "Hard Realities on an Innocent Nature," student essay, University of Massachusetts, Dartmouth, for Professor Wallin, 1991.

Epistemology, and the Stories of Nature." Environmental Ethics 18 (1996): 19-38.

Fairfax, Sally K., et al., *Buying Nature: The Limits of Land Acquisition as a Conservation Strategy, 1780-2004*, Cambridge, MA: The MIT Press 2005.

Fazzina, Nancy, "The Town Remains the Same," student essay, University of Massachusetts, Dartmouth, for Professor Wallin, 1991.

Fleck, Richard F., *Henry Thoreau and John Muir*, Hamden, CT: Archon Books 1985.

Fox, Stephen, *John Muir and His Legacy: The American Conservation Movement,* Little, Brown and Company, Boston, 1981.

Goodin, Robert, *Protecting the Vulnerable,* Chicago: University of Chicago Press, 1985.

Hallowell, Christopher and Levy, Walter, *Listening to Earth: A Longman Topics Reader,* NY: The Longman Publishing Group, 2005.

Hardin, Garrett, "The Tragedy of the Commons," Science, 162(1968): 1243-1248.

Hardin, Garrett, "Lifeboat Ethics: the Case Against Helping the Poor," Psychology Today, September 1974.

Holt, Lawrence, and Garvey, Diane, *The Wilderness Idea,* 58 minute video, Florentine Films, 1995.

Jackson, J. B., *Discovering the Vernacular Landscape,* New Haven: Yale University Press 1984.

Jackson, John Brinkerhoff, *The Westward Moving House in Landscapes,* ed. By Zube, Ervin. H., Amherst, MA: University of Massachusetts, 1970.

Johnson, Mark, *Moral Imagination: Implications of Cognitive Science for Ethics,* Chicago: University of Chicago, 1993.

Kaplan, Stephen and Rachel, *Humanscape: Environments for People,* Belmont, CA: Duxbury, 1982. republished by Ann Arbor, MI: Ulrich's, 1989.

Kaplan, Stephen and Rachel, *The Experience of Nature: a Psychological Perspective,* NY: Cambridge University Press, 1989, republished by Ann Arbor, MI: Ulrich's, 1995.

Kempton, Willet, et al., *Environmental Values in American Culture,* MIT Press, Cambridge, MA 1995.

Leopold, Aldo, *A Sand County Almanac, and sketches Here and There,* NY: Oxford University Press 1949.

Lopez, Barry, *The Stone Horse, in Crossing Open Ground*, NY: Vintage 1989.

McEvoy, Arthur F., "Toward an Interactive Theory of Nature and Culture: Ecology, Production, and Cognition in the California Fishing Industry," in Wooster, Donald, ed., *The Ends of the Earth: Perspectives on Modern Environmental History*, Cambridge UK: Cambridge University Press 1989.

McIntyre, Alistair, *After Virtue: A Study in Moral Theory*, Notre Dame, Indiana: Notre Dame University Press 1984; Johnson, Mark, The Moral Imagination: Implications of Cognitive Science for Ethics. Chicago: U of Chicago 1993.

Mendlesohn, Janet, *Figure in a Landscape*, 48 minute documentary, 1987, distributed by Direct Cinema Limited, Inc., P.O. Box 69799, Los Angeles, CA 90069.

Miller, James Edward, *The Transformation of the Political Process in Claiborne County, Mississippi*, Master of Regional Planning thesis, University of Massachusetts Amherst 1987.

Muir, John, *The American Wilderness: Essays by John Muir, Photographs by Ansel Adams*, edited by Barnes and Noble Books, introduction by Thaxton, John, New York: Barnes and Noble, 1993.

Norton, Bryan G., "The Constancy of Leopold's Land Ethic," *Environmental Pragmatism*, ed. Light, Andrew and Katz, Eric, NY: Routledge 1996.

O'Malley, Monica L., untitled student paper, University of Massachusetts Dartmouth, for Professor Wallin, 1991.

O'Neill, John, "The Varieties of Intrinsic Value," The Monist, vol. 75, #2, April 1992. *Ecology, Policy and Politics: Human Well-Being and the Natural World*, New York: Routledge, 1993.

Papineau, David, "The Tyranny of Common Sense," The Philosopher's Magazine, 2nd quarter, 20, 2006.

Pollan, Michael, *Second Nature*, New York: Grove Press, 2003.

Pratt, Mary Louise, *Imperial Eyes: Travel Writing and Transculturation*, London and NY: Routledge, 1992.

Raglon, Rebecca and Marian Scholtmeijer. "Shifting Ground: Metanarratives. Epistemology, and the Stories of Nature." Environmental Ethics 18 (1996): 19-38.

Ross, Andrew, *The Chicago Gangster Theory of Life: Nature's Debt to Society*, New York: Verso 1994.

Rybcinski, Withold, *Home: A Short History of an Idea*, New York: Viking Penguin, 1985.

Schama, Simon, *Landscape and Memory*, NY: Alfred A. Knopf 1995.

Schweder, Richard A., *Thinking Through Cultures*, Cambridge, MA: Harvard University Press 1991.

Signorello, Diana, "Lowell's Massachusetts Mill," student essay, University of Massachusetts, Dartmouth, for Professor Wallin, 1991.

Stone, Christopher D., *Should Trees have Standing? and other essays on Law, Morals, and the Environment*, 25th anniversary edition, Berkeley: University of Southern California Press, 1996.

Terborgh, John, *Where Have All the Birds Gone?: Essays on the Biology and Conservation of Birds That Migrate to the American Tropics*, Terborgh, Princeton: Princeton University Press, 1990.

Turner, Frederick, *Rediscovering America: John Muir in His Time and Ours*, Viking, NY, 1985.

von Wright, G. H., *The Varieties of Goodness*, NY and London: Routledge and Kegan Paul 1963, Ch. 3.

Walton, Linda D., *Creating Effective Schools for Minority Students*, Master of Regional Planning thesis, University of Massachusetts Amherst, 1988.

Wolff, Eric R., *Europe and the People Without History*, Los Angeles and Berkeley: University of California Press 1982.

Thanks

Heartfelt thanks to Eva Gordon, for wonderful editing; to Tyler Volk, author of *What is Death?*, *Gaia's Body*, and *Metapatterns*, for all the fine discussions since our faculty days at Manhattan's School of Visual Arts; to David and Sandy Williams, conservationists, adventurers, exemplars; to Marion McPhaul, for friendship and island conversation; to Julian and Adrian Ashford, for immersion in France on their organic farm; to Sena Jeter Naslund, author of *Ahab's Wife*, *Four Spirits*, and *Abundance*, for her friendship and longtime support of my work; to Ellie Bryant, author of *The Black Bonnet* and *Father by Blood*, for steady encouragement; to Dennis Pearson, Tom Newman, James Newman, Terry, Brownie, and Buddy Hairston, and Tommy Weeks, partners in experiencing the big woods; to Roy Hoffman, author of *Chicken Dreaming Corn*, for late night writing secrets; to Kaylene Johnson, author of *Portrait of the Alaska Railroad*, for spirit like her mountain west; to Betsy Woods, writer of bayou and heart, for sharing both; to Kathleen Driskell, author of *Laughing Sickness*, for support and co-editing, with Sena, the anthology *High Horse*; to Katy Yocum, for kindness and tiger revelations; to Karen Mann, for friendship and generous reading; to Ann Buttimer, author of *Sustainable Landscapes and Lifeways: Scale and Appropriateness*, for sharing geographic projects in teaching and publishing at University College Dublin; to Steve and Ellen Eder, dear friends and fine filmmakers whose Terra Nova documentaries have done so much; to Wendy Knight, for conceiving and editing *Far from Home*; to Lloyd Kelly, Jr., for endless ideas; to Jennifer Deane, for careful reading; to John Twomey, for many secrets of nature; to Jack & Beth Reed, woods neighbors with a complex forest view; to George Bonno Wenckebach, for the years of friendship and sailing; to Bob Yaro, Andy Scheffey, David Laws, Terry Blunt, and everyone from my time at the Regional Planning Program at the University of

Massachusetts Amherst; to Louise Habicht, Mike Lannon, Ray Dumont, Ed Thompson, Jerry Blitefield, Chris Eisenhart, Rick Hogan, Diane Barense, Phil Cox, Catherine Villaneuva Gardner, and all my supportive colleagues and students at the University of Massachusetts Dartmouth; to John Cook of the Nature Conservancy, for insight into the Malpai and other projects, and to Phoebe Cook and friends at the Sakonnet Preservation Association, for their dedication to preserving green acres; to Clyde Barrow and colleagues at the Center for Policy Analysis; and to Joyce McDonald and other colleagues and students at the Spalding University Master of Fine Arts in Writing Program; to Bonnelle Strickling, author of *Dreaming About the Divine*, for friendship and insights since the sixties; to Bill Moor, for fierce philosophical spirit; to Jennifer Sherlock and Anitra Carr for their enthusiasim, to Bryson Ley and Marsha Fretwell, Carolina comrades who conserve bodies and spirits; to Ivor Hanson, author of *Life on the Ledge*, and Christina Carlson, for warm friendship. I thank my wife Mary Elizabeth Gordon for the cover painting, design, editing, and many substantial ideas; Smoke, Clay, Rain, Brooks, and Eva, my children, and Sarah Wallin, my daughter-in-law, for lively interest and support; Skye, Cameron, Sierra, Talli, and Terra Sage, my grandchildren, whose mission, should they choose to accept it, is to apply the suggestions in this book. For financial support during various stages of this work I thank the J. William Fulbright Program, for my appointment at University College Dublin, Ireland, and I thank both the Sabbatical Leave Committee and the Provost's program of research grants of the University of Massachusetts Dartmouth. For design and technical support I thank John Souza and Melissa Jones; for formatting help I thank Richard Legault; for administrative support I thank Andrea Davis. Finally, most of all, I'm grateful to my mother, Ruth M. Wallin, for her love of the garden of nature, and to the memory of my father, Luther Wallin, Jr., who practiced sustainable forestry from the 1930s onward.

About the Author

Luke Wallin is Professor of English at the University of Massachusetts Dartmouth, and Senior Research Associate at the Center for Policy Analysis. He teaches in the Master of Fine Arts in Writing program at Spalding University.

More information is available at lukewallin.com.